ARS ALCHEMICA
FOUNDATIONS OF PRACTICAL ALCHEMY

FOUNDATIONS OF PRACTICAL ALCHEMY

ARS ALCHEMICA

BEING A PRIMA IN THE
PARACELSIAN ARTE OF SOLVE ET COAGULA

Gary St. M. Nottingham

Published by Avalonia
www.avaloniabooks.co.uk

Published by Avalonia
BM Avalonia, London, WC1N 3XX, England, UK
www.avaloniabooks.co.uk

ARS ALCHEMICA: FOUNDATIONS OF PRACTICAL ALCHEMY
© Gary St. M. Nottingham, 2016
All rights reserved.

First Paperback Edition, published by Avalonia, October 2016
ISBN 978-1-905297-98-6

Typeset and design by Satori
Photographs and artwork by Frances Nottingham and Gary St. M. Nottingham.

British Library Cataloguing in Publication Data. A catalogue record for this book is available from the British Library.

This book is sold subject to the condition that no part of it may be reproduced or utilized in any form or by any means, electronic or mechanical, including photocopying, microfilm, recording, or by any information storage and retrieval system, or used in another book, without written permission from the author.

Gary St. M. Nottingham

for F.M.N.

Other works by the author:

Foundations of Practical Sorcery

    Vol. I – Liber Noctis

    Vol. II – Ars Salomonis

    Vol. III – Ars Geomantica

    Vol. IV – Ars Theurgia Goetia

    Vol. V – Otz Chim

    Vol. VI – Ars Speculum

    Vol. VII – Liber Terriblis

About the Author

Gary St. M. Nottingham first came across alchemy when he was fifteen through reading the popular early 1970's occult magazine *'Man, Myth & Magic.'*

This encouraged him to find out further about the arte and to study Israel Regardie's 'The Philosopher's Stone'; this in turn led to the works of Hollandus, Paracelsus and eventually Junius. However, it was his involvement with a group of alchemical practitioners that opened many of the doors for him and much that he had learnt finally began to make sense.

Subsequently he has taught and written extensively on the alchemical arte, running several one-day workshops and weekends on practical laboratory alchemy.

His other areas of occult study are astrology, grimoires, and the Kabbalah, all of which are expressed as part of his alchemical work.

Table of Contents

INTRODUCTION 13

IN THE BEGINNING: BEING AN ACCOUNT OF THE
NECESSARY ATTITUDE UNTO THE ARTE.................................. 17

'SOLVE ET COAGULA, ET HABEBIS MAGISTERIAL': DISSOLVE
AND BIND AND YOU WILL THEN HAVE THE MAGISTERY 24

CONSIDERATIONS AND TIMING OF THE ARTE 37

MODUS & THE TOOLS OF ARTE THE PRACTICALITIES
OF ARTE.. 40

AQUA OPUS: THE WATER WORKS 65

THE SEVEN HELPERS: SEVEN PLANETARY TINCTURES............ 71

THE ELIXIR WORKINGS: THE ARTE OF SALT VOLATILIZATION . 81

VINI TARTARUS: WINE TARTAR AND ITS MYSTERY.................. 90

THE PRIMUM ENS: ACCESSING THE ESSENTIALS OF PLANTS.. 95

LAPIS VEGETABILIS AND THE CIRCULATUM MINOR: OF THE
VEGETABLE STONE BOTH LIQUID AND SOLID......................... 100

THE BHASMA: METALS AS MEDICINE 108

GEMSTONES: THE TINCTURES THEREOF 110

GLAUBER AND THE AURUM POTABLE: THE MEDICINE
OF THE SUN... 114

URANIA: INGRESS INTO THE LAPIS PHILOSOPHORUM............ 118

ESSENTIAL READING 128

INDEX.. 129

*To conquer without danger
Is to triumph without glory*
         ~ Fulcanelli   (20th century French Alchemist)

Disclaimer

This work is offered to the reader for its curiosity value only. Working with acids and hot objects can be dangerous, and the reader must consider the legality and suitability thereof.

*Ever mindful of that lunar spirit
From the Greater Key of Solomon*

Sophiel!

*Unto whom God in his wisdom
Did entrust
Such secret knowledge of both herb and stone*

The Fourth Pentacle of the Moon....

*'Defendeth thee from all evil sorceries
And from injury unto soul or body.
Its angel Sophiel, giveth the knowledge of the virtue
Of all herbs and stones and unto whomsoever
Shall name him he will procure the knowledge of all.'*

*'Let them be confounded who persecute me and
let me not be confounded;
let them fear and not I.'*

Introduction

Alchemy the Great Arte indeed the Royal Arte has held a fascination for mankind for all time, its imagery and symbols have been used by various people to try and describe their teachings on a wide array of mystical thoughts and deeds. Yet science would deny the arte and many would consider it to be little more than a superstitious trifle, something belonging to another age. However therein lies its safety, as others dismiss it and decry the students and practitioners thereof as being foolish. They, the critics, have put in place their own barriers which impedes their understanding not only of the arte itself but the wider mysteries of life. And as such alchemy has survived centuries of persecution, particularly in the early centuries of Christianity, when the great alchemical minds of Alexandria were persecuted and the arte went underground. Yet it didn't quite go away, enough survived the centuries to create a modern renaissance and this work hopefully will contribute something to this.

During 1972 I was reading a copy of the old occult magazine *Man, Myth & Magic* which contained an article concerning the work of a modern alchemist; at the time this fired my imagination and the romance of the mystery has always stayed with me. Later I discovered Regardie's alchemical work *The Philosopher's Stone,* of which I could make no sense, and thus it was many years before I found ingress into the arte.

Some years later I read Manfred Junius's work on spagyrics, this at last was a way into the arte, however it wasn't long before I realised that there were major keys being left out. As a practitioner of the wider field of the Western Magical Traditions I sought to remedy this deficit by the conjuration of grimoire spirits to aid in rectifying this. Subsequently I performed a conjuration of the spirit Sophiel from the Greater Key of Solomon to aid me and assist me with my alchemical undertaking. The work appeared to produce no phenomena at the time and I considered it a failure, but decided to use the experience as a dry run and repeat it the following full moon. However events took over and I didn't follow this up and half forgot about the working. Nine weeks later to the day, (nine being significant as the number of the moon) I was attending an occult conference and an elderly American approached out me of a crowded hall and asked if I was interested in alchemy, I was a surprised at this but agreed to meet up the next day. Perhaps he didn't think that I'd be there, I wasn't certain whether he would be either, it all seemed so unusual... then I remembered the working previously, checked the date that it was nine weeks previously and realised that this was a manifestation of the working and it wasn't a failure at all. This fired me with new vigour. True to his word the gentleman was there waiting for me, subsequently we had lunch and a long discussion on alchemy and he came back home to continue the work. Before he left next day he put me in touch with somebody who had been hosting alchemical weekends at their manor house on the edge of Dartmoor to which, at a later date, I was invited. My first meeting was the following May: I was met at the railway station in Exeter, from where I was chauffeured across Devon to God knows where on the edge of Dartmoor. I remember coming around the corner of an overgrown lane and entering a short drive which suddenly ended at a large rambling manor house. Outside were parked several very expensive cars and the whole atmosphere was like something out of Dennis Wheatley's novel *The Devil Rides Out*. I was more intrigued than apprehensive and thought that this was not the average pagan moot! Having been introduced to some twenty people, many from various parts of the world, the weekend started with a couple of lectures and meditations. Great stuff... then the lab works followed!

I consider myself very fortunate to have had such an introduction to the arte and not one that many students are likely to receive. During my time at this event much was discussed and demonstrated, contacts made, and knowledge gleaned.

This work is in appreciation of that time.

G. St. M. Nottingham on the eve of the feast of St Antony
2016

CHAPTER ONE

In the Beginning: Being an account of the necessary attitude unto the arte

In the beginning we must appreciate the depth and enormity of the alchemical artes; for the arte is no mere exercise in the psychological or sexual speculation of the nature of the soul. However the soul of the alchemist cannot but be affected by the arte, and indeed to be successful with the higher works one must have developed a psychic and spiritual perception of creation and also of one's place therein.

Whilst the terminology of alchemy easily lends itself to the methods of exploration of the hinterlands of the soul, as demonstrated by Jung, alchemy is primarily a laboratory work; which in turn is highly influenced by astrology, kabbalistic concepts and ritual magic. To gain any proficiency in our arte all these occult disciplines and more will be called into action.

Underlying our arte is the hermetic view of the unity of all life, the grandeur of creation and the magical view that we and everything therein is but an expression thereof. We can approach the higher worlds via the lower and this is something which alchemy will help to do. By taking a plant, mineral or metal the alchemist can by the demands and working of the arte bring its potency to the fore; and thus, aided by these, their allies of the arte, they are enabled to approach the starry realms.

In the beginning, as the Bible's Book of John would have it, 'The word was with God,' and thus everything in creation becomes an expression thereof; and we can find the same concept within the Holy Kabbalah; that is, out of nothing come all things. Therefore every act and deed must ultimately be an expression of Divinity, regardless of whether we, as individuals, find it comfortable or not. We are not here because the universe owes us a living or indeed an easy time, neither are we here so that our emotional and physical needs are daily met to our satisfaction, these needs and wants indeed change as we gain more experience of life. We are here to experience life in its entirety, we are here as an expression of a Divinity that unfolds and knows itself, we are here because we are. All cultures at some time have tried to make sense of this condition and come to terms with it, some being more successful than others. Within the Western culture, despite the suppression by Christianity, the esoteric traditions have always been present, although barely discernible.

However deep within the monastic traditions of Christianity the alchemical and occult traditions managed to survive the persecutions, with the Benedictine order being particularly worthy of note in the saving and surreptitious promotion of these artes. One only has to consider the likes of Trithemius the German abbot of a Benedictine abbey who was highly influential upon Agrippa and also upon Paracelsus. The 15th century alchemical master George Ripley was also of the order of St Benedict and of course - as legend tells us - Sir Edward Kelley found the red powder of transmutation at the Benedictine abbey of Glastonbury.

Despite Christian suppression of the occult, the arte survived owing to the secret activities of some of its adherents who saved and worked with alchemical and magical texts; and it is to these astute brothers of the arte that we owe our thanks.

It was Theophrastus Bombastus von Hohenheim better known as Paracelsus (1493-1541) who was the greatest expounder of the spagyric arte and who based many of his medicinal preparations upon its practices. The word spagyric is considered to be from two Greek words spao – to draw out, or to divide and agerio – to gather together or bind together; which succinctly describes the modus operandi involved, namely the breaking down, purifying, exalting and then rejoining the component parts together in the alchemical marriage, thus promoting and liberating the potency of the herb, mineral or metal in question. These spagyrical confections can be en-hallowed by magical and meditative procedure, thus deepening and making more subtle their potencies.

The spagyrical arte, whilst part of the alchemical corpus, is often referred to as the Lesser Work and is considered to be of profound importance in approaching the higher works of transmutation. As the spagyrical work prepares the student and teaches important procedures such as calcination, distillation and the mysteries of the Chymical Wedding, spagyrics in its own right is worthy of study and stands as a part of the magical corpus.

It is from the temples of Egypt and also the Gnostic and Hermetic schools of the early centuries A.D. that western alchemy was birthed.

Amongst the accessible European texts that have survived, particular note must be made of the writings of Paracelsus, as these are relevant to our work and its author is easily identified. This is not the case with many alchemical texts. The whole language of alchemy and the imagery thereof is highly elusive as it draws upon metaphorical and mythological thinking; but once understood the images become clearer as we realise to what it is they are alluding to.

Therefore to be an alchemist, one must understand the imagery, but you can only understand this if you are an alchemist; thus entry into the Garden of the Philosophers is not for all, as it becomes an initiation into the arte as one's experience unfolds. Our alchemical work takes place in three stages, namely separation, purification and cohabitation, aso known as recombining, or the chymical wedding. It is these practices that increase and release the potency of the gemstone, herb or metallic ore. Herbal teas and tinctures, whilst having a long and noble history will only make use of some of the plant's potencies; much will be thrown away. Thus the spagyrical arte will open up the plant and grant access to its power. Just as homeopathy has its modus which science cannot comprehend so do the spagyrical artes. Whilst the herbalist will discard the plant remains after they have been used in teas and tinctures, the spagyricist will extract the life force, oils and salts, purify them and when exalted will then recombine them. It is the 'Terra Damnata', that is the damned earth, that which is left over, which is then discarded. These are the essentials which carry the life force, the consciousness and body of the substance which is being worked upon. Within the arte these three principles are known as:

- Mercury...The carrier of the life force, this is alcohol in the vegetable kingdom.

- Sulphur... The consciousness, and is the volatile plant oils and also a fixed salt which is known as the sal sulphurous
- Salt...The plant salts which are extracted after the body has been destroyed by fire and resurrected.

The spagyricist will find it useful to also take into consideration the astrology of the working; that is, what is happening to the planet that governs the plant in question; is it helped or hindered by the moon? If the planet is badly aspected then it would be prudent to wait until the adverse aspect has passed. With slower moving planets this can take a while before this happens. If the planet is retrograde, that is, it appears to be travelling backwards through the zodiac, this will also hinder the work. Also of import will be the day and the hour thereof too. Whilst it can be difficult to match all favourable conditions, if the moon makes a good aspect to the planet that rules the herb then I would advise the use of that day, preferably in the hour of the planet that governs the herb, this shouldn't be too onerous.

These factors can help or hinder the work and this will become more apparent with the higher workings. As your work reflects the state of the heavens one needs to be mindful of the hermetic dictum *'as above, so below.'* The heavenly bodies are themselves transmitters of a higher energy which will have an effect on all aspects of life and also on all things which are in existence, whether this is recognised or not. Subsequently the flow of the cosmic tides can help or hinder any attempts to bring operations of the arte unto perfection, or indeed any activity in any sphere of life.

All matter has an intelligence and a personality, although we may not be aware of them as such. Nonetheless we can work with them, by firstly recognising that they exist and acknowledging them. This will be a start, for such an attitude will help promote a successful conclusion to the work. All matter is alive at its own level, and developing an awareness of this fact is important to the arte.

As Paracelsus reminds us:

> '...Thus your medicine bears its fruits as the summer bears its fruits.
> You must know that the summer does this with the help of the stars
> not without them. If the stars are able to do this, you must know how
> the medicine is prepared in this way and that it is ruled by the stars.
> For it is they that complete the work of the physician.
> And since it is they that act, the medicine must be understood,
> classified and adjusted to their influence.
> Therefore you must understand that the medicine must be prepared in the stars and that the stars become the medicine.'

A second consideration is the emotional and psychic state of the spagyricist, for as the purer and the more refined the matter which is being worked upon becomes, it will become more susceptible to the psychic energies of the alchemist. Therefore the alchemist must abandon any negative states of mind, and must be fully concentrated upon the work in hand and not distracted by any irrelevant thoughts or conversation. The Benedictine adept Basilius Valentinus (also known as Basil Valentine) says in his alchemical work that:

> '...In this my consideration, I have actually found five points, which are the noblest and which all seekers of wisdom and lovers of the arte are in duty bound to inquire into.
> first there is the invocation of God;

second the consideration of nature;
third the true unadulterated preparation;
fourth the application
and fifth the usefulness.
These five points then every chymicus and true alchemist must know how to consider and recognise.
For otherwise without it he cannot be perfect,
nor be completely recognised as a true spagirum.'

However you may perceive divinity or by what traditions you hold it sacred, the invocation of the highest, and the blessing by the spagyricist of the work in hand, are of paramount importance and must precede the work. It will be also advantageous to proceed with a short meditation on the work and its goals. Once these have been completed the working can now progress, for as the good monk would tell us 'the good must be separated from the bad.'

CHAPTER TWO

'Solve et Coagula, et habebis magisterial': Dissolve and bind and you will then have the magistery

The arte considers any physical object, be it animal, mineral or vegetable, to be a combination of the four elements. Air, fire, and water are combined to produce the fourth element, earth. Thus the element earth becomes the form for the other three elements to manifest. The arte requires that this form must be destroyed which will then allow the liberation of the other three elements, this is dissolution. Fire being sulphur, air is thus mercury and salt is associated with water.

Here we have the three mother letters of the Holy Kabbalah: shin = fire, aleph = air and mem = water. As colour is associated within alchemy with light and heat, it is therefore considered to be a manifestation of fire; whilst the mercury is deemed to be of the air, as it is volatile and is perceived as a gas. The attribution of the salt to water owes much to the fact that alchemical salts, when pure, will suck water out of the atmosphere and this fact is the key to much of the arte, as will be explained in due course.

Furthermore these three principles can be seen in the following kabbalistic thinking with the salt equating with the Nephesh; that is the lower self. This is the animal part of one's being, the body and its animal needs which must be brought to heel and come under the dominion of the higher consciousness. Mercury is associated with the Ruach, the objective faculty and becomes the vehicle for the spirit which encompasses the individual consciousness. And sulphur is considered to be of the Neschamah and is seen as the outer expression of the higher consciousness. Thus alchemical principles are expressed throughout all of nature. According to the alchemical corpus the manifestation of matter is maintained through the co-operation of these three essentials, mercury, sulphur and salt. In alchemy these are the Holy Trinity, the Three in One and One in Three. In alchemical terminology their meanings are:

Mercury: ☿

Within the vegetable kingdom this is seen as the life principle which is carried by the alcohol. As it is never free in nature the alcohol only comes into being when the plant material breaks down and starts to ferment; thus it is created by the fermentation of the plant material whereby mercury is considered to be birthed and solely to be used with that particular plant as it has absorbed the plant's life force. This is known as the 'long path' and is considered the most superior method. However, if the alcohol is from the red grape then this mercury will be deemed suitable for use in any workings of the vegetable kingdom instead of fermenting the actual plant material. If it is digested with the sal ammoniac (an ammonium salt) it will be suitable for workings within the mineral and metallic realms as well. By circulating the mercury over its own salt it will become imbued with the life forces of creation. This mercury is seen as being feminine and passive, sometimes referred to as the White Wife or White Queen. It is also known as Diana and is represented by the astrological symbol for Mercury.

The Mercury of the plant kingdom, being ethyl alcohol, ethanol, (C_2H_5OH) always carries within it the life principle and this form of alcohol must never be confused with other forms such as methyl alcohol, or any other alcohols as these can be fatal. As alcohol is never found free within nature it must be fermented and subsequently distilled and having been distilled it is then re-distilled several times to remove excess water; this operation is called rectification; and is often referred to in old alchemical texts as *'letting seven eagles fly.'* This is because the spirit of the alcohol is volatile and will evaporate if it is heated, leaving any impurities behind. When the water is removed the mercury/alcohol will be considered to have been dried off and will be nearly 100% pure. However removing all the water is not easy as the alcohol will absorb water from the atmosphere as it is hydroscopic. The best that you will probably be able to achieve will be a distillate of 97%. This level will be suitable for all spagyric preparations. If the alcohol is digested with potassium carbonate (which can be acquired from wood ash or best of all from calcined vine prunings), the last remaining water will be removed. Salt from wine tartar is good for this too as it is of a universal vegetable origin.

When a liquid is placed in a container three things will hold it in situ, namely gravity, molecular bonds and air pressure. If any or one of these are weakened then the state of the fluid will change, therefore when the liquid is heated in a distillation train or glass retort the heat will cause the water molecules to move faster and this in turn will weaken the bonds that hold them all together. Therefore the water molecules will arise as a vapour and will travel through the flask and condense upon the colder surfaces and return back to water. If this is collected in another flask this will be the distilled water and all impurities will have been left behind. As liquids boil and evaporate at different temperatures this will allow them to be separated from any impurities which are present, therefore as alcohol boils at 78°c and water at 100°c we can with patience easily separate the two liquids.

With the first distillation do not go over 85°c as you will be encouraging too much water to come over. Some of the water molecules will come over with the alcohol as will also other impurities and toxins; and these will have to be removed too. Even when holding the temperature at 78°c some water will manage to come over with the alcohol. The alcohol-water mix from this distillation is now redistilled and that which distils at 76°c and under is discarded as this will hold various toxins, which obviously we do not want. Carrying on with the distillation the alcohol will probably be 90% pure and with further gentle distillations this will increase. When the alcohol has all been distilled over, the temperature in the flask will have risen which is a good sign that the alcohol has been separated from the fluids. The cloudy water that is left behind in the flask is the phlegm and this will be used for further operations of the arte. However do not distil over or near an open flame as the alcohol will catch fire and you do not want to burn down your home!

There are various methods of avoiding this which are known to the practitioner of this arte. One of course is to use a heating mantle; these are not cheap but are very good and reliable as the temperature can easily be set and maintained. Also a hot plate is good and reliable but these can be expensive, but I have had good results from using two ringed electric hotplates which can be bought from high street stores even car boot sales and charity shops.

Sulphur: 🜍

This is the consciousness of the plant and carries its personality, it is also deemed to be the soul of the plant. It is present within the volatile oils and so also is a fixed salt which is extracted from the dregs of the distilled plant, which is referred to as the fixed salts of sulphur, or the *sal sulphuris*. The soul, the sulphur will unite the Mercury with the body as the mercury and salt do not mix. It is the soul that enables the spirit, the life force to manifest within the body, the salt. The sulphur is seen as being a male who has an active and fiery nature and is thus referred to as Apollo or the Sun or as The Red King.

The oils are easily extracted by passing steam through the plant material and collecting the water as the steam condenses, with the plant oils then floating on the top of the water. In alchemical texts we sometimes see this being expressed as the king, which is the sulphur/oil, swimming on a sea. The plant material is placed in the flask and the flask is half filled with water which is then left for several hours to soak. This will help break down the plant's cellular structure and help the oils to be released. The fluid is now brought to the boil and the steam as it rises will carry the plant oils over with it. The water is collected in a separating funnel; the oils which will be floating upon the top of the fluid can now easily be separated by draining the water off the oils. If these oils are re-distilled they will give a pure plant sulphur. However not all plants have a high oil content; plants such as fennel, lavender, rosemary and thyme have a much higher oil content than lemon balm.

The liquids that are left over in the flask are now poured into a large dish, a saucepan will be ideal for this; and this is now heated but not boiled; it will be preferable to perform this operation outside. A black tar will form and this must now be burnt. This is calcination and can take several hours to perform., because of this you may not be able to do it in one session. A camping stove is good for this, as is a blow torch. Slowly the ashes will become grey; these ashes will hold the fixed salts of the sulphur. The ashes must now be placed in a flask and distilled water poured over them. Stand the flask somewhere warm for several hours and occasionally agitate it, the salts will thereby be leached out of the ash. Pour the water through a funnel which has been plugged with cotton wool; this will allow the pure dissolved salts to pass through within the water.

When the water is gently evaporated the salt will appear as pale crystals; and these crystals will need to be re-calcined. The dissolution and washing process is then repeated to increase the purity of the salts. If the salts are washed with a mixture of distilled water which has had some distilled red wine vinegar poured into it then they will become even whiter, vinegar being the fixed mercury of the vegetable kingdom.

Salt: ⊖

The salt is the body and is prepared from the burning, the calcinations, of the plant material. The salts are extracted from the ash and by the demands of the arte they are purified and will become white. When this happens they are the outer form of the material which will hold the mercury and sulphur.

Once the mercury and the sulphur have been extracted from the plant material, the plant is burnt and it will give off a lot of smoke so this is best done outside. As was previously explained the salts are extracted through digesting the ash with distilled water, and the water being filtered is then distilled off, which will leave the salts behind. Both salts - the sulphur salts and the plant body salts - are ground fine and then mixed together; these salts will need to be kept dry. On the days of the waxing moon the salts must be exposed to the night air, preferably outside or at least near an open window. The salts will start to absorb the moisture out of the air and as they do will also absorb the life force that is carried in the atmosphere, which is also known as chi, prana or, in the alchemical traditions, the secret fire.

This energy is at its most potent in the spring time when everything is renewing itself; which can also be seen in the imagery from the alchemical text *Liber Mutus*, where the two figures which are collecting the early morning dew, show that the ram and the bull are present. This is an indication of the astrological signs Aries and Taurus which are the spring time signs. It also shows that both the moon and sun are present indicating the full moon. Therefore the best time would be on a waxing moon nearer full and when the sun is domiciled in the signs of Aries or Taurus. In the morning the salts must be covered up and not exposed to sunlight; they can be left out again the following night. In the Emerald Tablet it is declared that *'the sun is its father and the moon its mother and the wind carries it in its belly.'* It is this process which its author Hermes Trismegistus is referring to.

The moisture can be gently distilled off the salts and this water will then be the *aqua angelus*, the angel water. The salts are then re-introduced back into the water and gently digested somewhere warm, and then distilled off again. This act will set the secret fire within the salts. If these salts are left in the angel water for several weeks to digest they will become volatile, which is needed for higher spagyrical works such as plant stones. The secret of alchemically volatilizing salts is generally something which is passed on orally and not written down; there are other methods which will be explained.

Thus the Mercury and the Salt, which are in opposition to one another - that is, Spirit and Matter, which will not mix together – are, through the action of the Sulphur, allowed to co-exist. The sulphur will allow the mercury to marry with the salt and the three will then become one; the One in Three or the Chymical Wedding.

Operations of Arte

Fermentation:

The act of fermentation is the key that opens the secrets of Nature, which is why it is an important operation of the arte. If plant material is placed in a clean bucket with distilled water and kept warm it will undergo fermentation and will create a small amount of alcohol. Some plants have more natural sugars than others so the alcohol yield will be more. The fresh material that is being fermented will have its own natural yeast spores upon it which should be sufficient for the work in hand. Sometimes the alchemist will assist this operation by adding sugar at 200gms per litre and a little wine yeast to the mix (which is known as the must) thus allowing for a more vibrant fermentation which will give an increase in the alcohol content. For the first three days stir the must daily, this will allow the air above the fermentation to be renewed as any stagnation will impede the yeast development.

After the third day the build-up of carbon dioxide above the must will help to promote the development of the alcohol content. Check the alcohol content with a hydrometer and when fermentation has finished, decant the liquid off the solids and leave to settle. When clear, usually within a week or two, it can be distilled. Discard all liquid which comes over at 76°c or less as this will contain toxins such as methyl alcohol which under no circumstances do we want as drinking it can impair both your eyesight and your health, therefore it is important that it is eliminated. The alcohol will need to be rectified and all water removed as far as possible.

Philosophic Distillation:

If we now evaporate off all liquids that are left in the flask after we have distilled the alcohol we will have remaining a dark tarry mass which is full of alchemical properties which we require such as the sal ammoniac. Therefore pour our alcohol back over this and distil off again, do this seven times and our alcohol will become enriched. It can also be circulated over this 'honey' by adding an aludel to the flask giving it more room to expand. If you do this then place the flask somewhere warm for a week so that it can gently evaporate and condense against the cold sides of the flask thus allowing it to run back down and to repeat itself; this operation is known to the arte as circulation. The alcohol will now be considered to be a 'Philosophical Mercury of the Vegetable Kingdom.'

Figure 1: From the Liber Mutus

Calcination:

If you use the vegetable material which has undergone an extraction via alcohol this will be highly inflammable so be careful. If you are calcining the plant material in a crucible with no lid then it will go no higher that 400-500°c which is sufficient for our work. Once the ash starts to turn grey place a lid on the crucible if you haven't done so already as salts will start to sublimate and our work requires the more volatile salt. In higher plant workings such as the circulatum or plant stone then salts which have either been volatilised or have been fused through very high heat will be needed to grant success.

Circulation:

We have already touched upon this operation, however it can be seen as a continuous act of distillation in which the distillate falls back into the liquid that is being distilled. This is an operation that will enrich the menstrum in the more volatile components such as the sal ammoniac that will allow the vegetable mercury to bond with all. This can be done via the pelican or the two brothers, although aludels and condensers on flasks will work well even just a very large flask with lots of room in it will be adequate for this operation.

Digestion:

Digestion is not the same as maceration although they share some points in common. However this takes place ideally in a flask with a long neck and the flask is sealed. The flask is kept at a temperature between 15-20°c and as there is no yeast then there will be no fermentation. The process can continue for several weeks or indeed months as the contents gradually open to the alchemical attributes which will be present.

Figure 2: Alchemical pelican

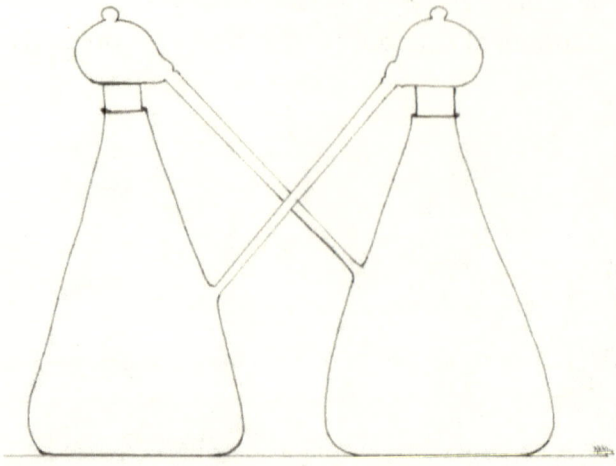

Figure 3: The two brothers

Cohabitation:

This is the Coagula of 'Solve et Coagula' and is where the purified elements of the work are recombined, where the alchemical marriage takes place. This occurs when the alchemically prepared Sulphur, Mercury and Salt are reunited and is a delicate operation as foreign bodies and rogue sulphurs can ruin the result, therefore cleanliness is of importance. After cohabitation the material can endure a long digestion as the components marry together.

Imbibition:

This is part of the creation of alchemical stones; the salt which is the body is fed with the sulphur and the mercury drop by drop over many weeks. The amount of liquid that is used is minimal as the work will be ruined if it is flooded. Imbibition takes place on the planetary day and hour that is relevant to the work. Afterwards the work is placed somewhere warm to digest, when the surface stops drying out then it will take no more.

CHAPTER THREE

Considerations and timing of the arte

'Nothing can succeed without a favoured moon'

Agrippa

The alchemical arte is greatly influenced both by the state of the stars and the practitioner; success being more likely when adequate preparations have been made and the heavens favour the work. If a planet which governs the herb, metal or mineral is badly aspected then success will be difficult to achieve. Often this will manifest as accidents, interruptions at critical times, or simply the dropping of a flask which has taken months to prepare; by contrast, when the heavens favour the working, success is more likely to be within reach. With many works published on the magical workings of plant and stone, it can be perplexing when these texts seem to give conflicting accounts of the astrological potencies of these beings. Without doubt I would suggest that one confers with Culpeper's Herbal as he was both an astrologer and herbalist; although he was rather fixed in his views he knew what he was on about when it came to astrology and plants and in my opinion he is second to none.

The alchemist needs to be focused upon the work; prayer, meditation and magical workings can all be used with advantage in helping to attune the practitioner unto the working in hand. It is of note that Daniel Schulke, writing in the work *Ars Philtron*, suggests that the cleanliness of body, mind and instruments is of great import. He also advises avoidance of both alcohol and sexual activity as ... *'these prohibitions are of incalculable value, chiefly for the homeostasis of the Aethyric Body as a precondition for the Art Magical, as well as a gesture of devotion and respect.'*

Whilst he gives a clear regimen for the harvesting of plant material, many of these protocols are also expressed by Chris Zalewski in her work *'Herbs in Magic and Alchemy.'* Whereby she suggests several rites and magical gestures that endeavour to connect with the spirit of the plant that is being worked with; it is clear that the plant spirit then becomes an ally who will aid the success of the working. Such an approach will lift the workings beyond the world of mere chemistry and the alchemist becomes a player in the great expression of life as the work unfolds.

How the moon aspects the planets will also be of importance. With the waxing moon, and the increasing lunar tide, the potency of the plant increases and the tides of the unseen worlds will flow with the work. The time from the new moon until the first quarter is an ideal time for the birthing of most projects. At the full moon the energy currents are peaking and is a good time to allow for the completion of any projects; although the waning moon and particularly the last quarter are good for the creation of banishing works as the magical artes will declaim.

All glassware that is acquired and anything else that is to be used within the arte is to be blessed by formulating simple rites of one's own devising; if intent is present then the outer form of this work need not be too complex. It is this marking the work out from the everyday which will help to en-hallow the operations of the arte and will then lift both the alchemist and the work far above the mundane.

As the work is easily affected by states of mind and other peoples' vibes all negativity is to be kept out of the laboratory as far as possible, for this is to be considered a holy place and the profane must be kept at bay. The higher the works the more this dictum must be observed, such menstrums as alcohol or even distilled water will easily absorb the energies of other peoples' thoughts and thus will pollute your efforts. They may not mean to do so but it will be the case if you cannot shield the work; the creation of astral guards to the laboratory will be no bad thing as you will soon realise.

CHAPTER FOUR

Modus & the Tools of Arte
The practicalities of Arte

Familiarity with laboratory glassware and praxis is of paramount importance, the siting of the laboratory will also need some thought.

Simple matters such as ventilation will need attention; good lighting and a water supply will be required; you will also need plenty of benching and shelving. Such glassware as bends, condensers, flasks, retorts and soxhlet extractors are easy enough to come by although, unless you have some familiarity with their use, it may take you a little while to become used to them.

Flasks:

These come in all sizes, the most useful will be round bottom flasks with a socket size B29. The sizes that you will require will be 1L, 500ml and 250ml. Also flat bottom flasks as above will be needed.

Round bottom flask:

These flasks are needed for heating mantles however they are also manufactured with a flat bottom which is needed if you are using a hotplate as they can stand upon it.

Figure 4: Round bottom flask

Retorts:

These will probably have to be made to order, although sometimes you can find them on eBay. They are needed for such workings as the volatilization of plant salts when making elixirs. They are also useful for the distillation of alcohol from red wine and for the production of distilled waters.

Condensers:

These are glass tubes which can vary in size and have an outside glass jacket through which cold water runs. This will allow that which is being distilled to condense against a cold surface. The tubing which carries the water will need to be connected to an aquarium pump in a bucket of water. This will allow it to work for days at a time with little attention. Condensers are often connected to soxhlets as part of the extraction process.

Figure 5: Glass retort

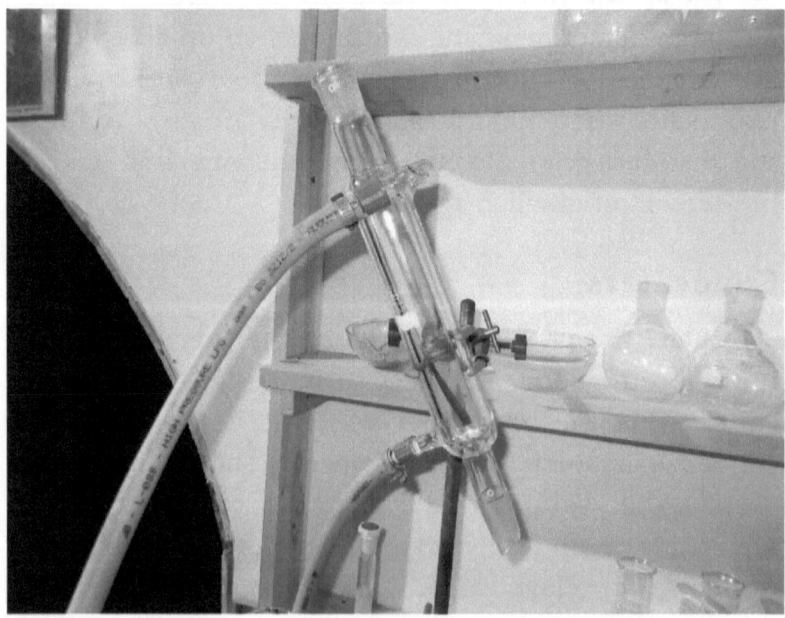

Figure 6: Condenser: cold water enters at the bottom and exits at the top

Soxhlet Extraction:

This is an ingenious confection as it allows for rapid high-quality extraction of the potencies of the herb. The herb is placed in a paper thimble; unbleached coffee filters are good for this.

The soxhlet is connected to a flask and the menstrum therein will evaporate and condense upon the cold surface of the condenser, this drops back into the soxhlet, as this fills with the herb-laden menstum the properties are quickly extracted and will be siphoned off into the original flask below. From here it will repeat the operation again and again. When the menstrum in the soxhlet becomes clear it is a sign that the properties of the plant material have been extracted.

Heat Source:

Probably the best and safest means of heat will be heating mantles and hotplates. These are not cheap, although hotplates can be bought from Argos at reasonable prices, heating mantles are really ideal as they can be left working for days. Both sources of heat can be controlled and I would advise their use particularly when you are working with anything that is inflammable, such as alcohol or acetone. Camping stoves are also useful particularly when calcining plant material, however you will need to keep an eye on them when in use and never use them with anything that is inflammable.

Bends, Connectors and Measuring Cylinders:

Make sure that your bends and the connectors are all the same size and will fit your flask sockets. Measuring cylinders should also be glass as this is easier to clean. Such things as stoppers, thermometers, clamps and stands are all self-explanatory. Still heads will allow your flask to be used for distillation as it will also take a thermometer, which will allow for easier control of the temperature.

Figure 7: Soxhlet: condenser fits on the top of the soxhlet

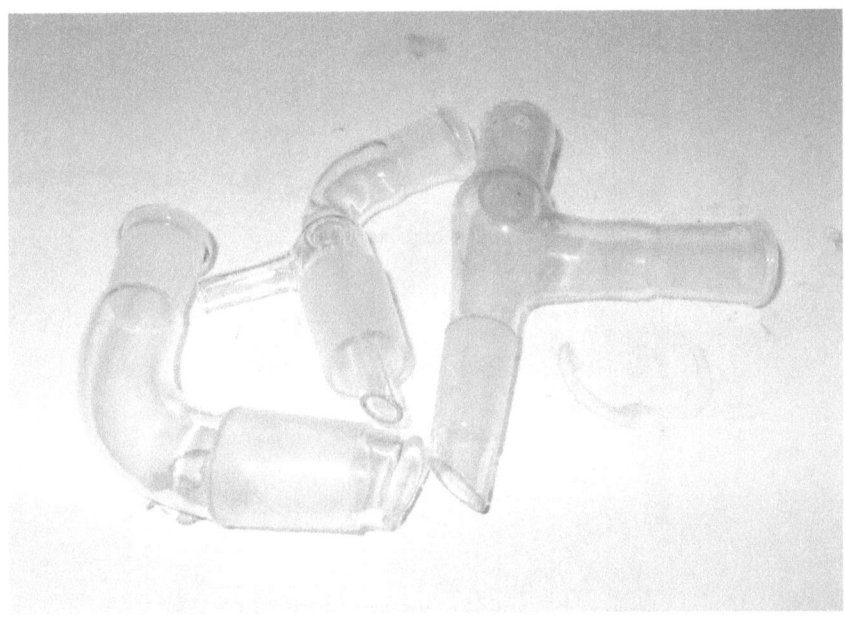

Figure 8: Glass bends

Figure 9: Distillation head

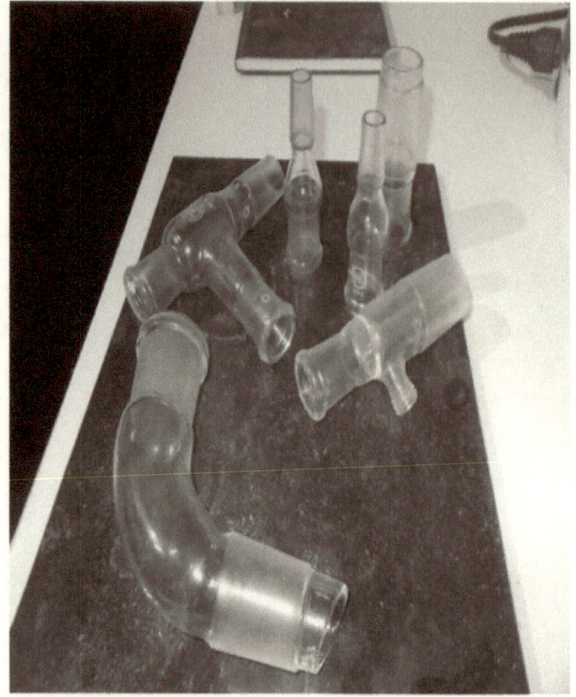

Figure 10: Joints allowing different size glassware to connect

Figure 11: Measuring cylinders

Pelicans:

Again you will need to have one made. They are similar to two round flasks joined together with two hollow arms that connect the top flask with the bottom one. This allows the liquid to gently distil and condense so that they then run back down into the bottom of the flask. By performing this operation for days at a time the menstrum will become more potent.

Figure 12: Pelican: this will have to be specially made

Aludels:

These are round flasks which have an entrance at each end which allows them to be joined together in a chain if need be. They are used as the pelican in the circulation and digestion of our menstrums.

Figure 13: Two aludels working together.
These will need to be made to order

The Menstrua:

These are the various menstrums that are used within the arte to dissolve and extract the properties of various materials. The mercury of each of the realms is a suitable menstrum for the working in that particular kingdom. Thus for the vegetable kingdom alcohol is the volatile mercury and vinegar the fixed mercury. An Alkahest is a menstrum which is capable of extracting a particular aspect of the material, for example some alkahests will extract the oils, or the sulphur, from gemstones and these can be created from the fixed and volatile mercuries of the vegetable kingdom with the addition of sal ammoniac. As alcohol, being a volatile mercury, is liberated through distillation; vinegar spirit, being the fixed mercury of the vegetable kingdom, is freed from red wine vinegar via the processes of freezing and then distilling.

Water is also used as a menstrum and is often combined with alcohol to form a vegetable menstrum that will quickly extract the properties of plants. The water must be distilled before use and if you are using tap water should be distilled at least twice to remove impurities. Water that is distilled from rainwater is excellent and even better is water which has been collected during a thunderstorm as this will be charged with the life force of nature. Another water which is good to work with is dew, this is not easy to collect and can only be collected before sunrise between the spring equinox and the summer solstice. It can be collected by dragging a clean towel over short grass which is then wrung out into a bucket. If you pin a towel onto a piece of wood and then tie a rope onto the wood you can easily drag it across the ground.

This method is demonstrated in Armand Barbault's work *'Gold of a Thousand Mornings.'* As the dew has been in contact with plant material it is best used only in the vegetable kingdom. Upon collection, the dew can be distilled and if the dregs are calcined, they will produce a white salt which is used in higher alchemical workings.

A final menstrum is the Oleum Tartari, oil of tartar. This is used in the Primum Ens and will be explored accordingly.

These menstrums are considered to be living beings, and as they become more refined through distillation are easily influenced by the psychic state of the alchemist for better or worse.

Preparation of our Vegetable Mercury

Water boils at 100°c and if we catch the steam against a cold surface it will condense and then return back to water. By doing so it will leave any impurities behind and even when using clean-looking water you will be surprised at what may get left behind in the flask. Alcohol will boil at 78°c, a much lower temperature than water, thus we are able to separate it from red wine quite easily. Do not fill the flasks any more than two-thirds full, as this will allow room for any slight expansion and bubbling of the fluid as it heats. Alcohol, our vegetable mercury, will contain toxins which must be removed and as these will distil over at 64°c and above it will be prudent to discard the first 10% of the distillate as this will be of no use and will be toxic.

For the first distillation, 80-85°c will bring over the alcohol much faster, but it will contain a lot of water that will have come over with it. This can be lessened by the use of a vigeraux column which allows the water droplets to condense on the inner glass and drop back into the liquid being distilled; while useful it is not necessary. When you have collected the first distillation it must then be redistilled; maintaining the temperature at 78-80°c. This is rectification and will concentrate the alcohol further. This can be repeated further again as the water will attach itself to the alcohol and some will again come over in the distillate, therefore the alcohol must be redistilled another three or four times; each time becoming purer.

Whilst 100% will be ideal this will not be possible as the alcohol itself will attract moisture to itself when it is exposed to the air. However it is not wise to distil in a completely enclosed distillation train as this can explode with the pressure that will build up in the system; therefore some means to let some of the pressure escape will be required. If the resultant alcohol is poured over some warm potassium carbonate salts, (pot carb) this will remove any water that remains in the alcohol and by doing this you can produce an alcohol, our vegetable mercury, with a purity of 98-99%. However, the best pot carb is produced from wine tartar, (more later) or from calcined vine prunings or from oak ash. If you do use commercial pot carb (which will be considered to be dead) you must first calcine it for an hour and then dissolve it in distilled rainwater and then evaporate the water. This will cause the potassium carbonate salts to reappear. If these are then left outside at night to deliquesce for several nights and then dried off they will be fit to use instead of the wine tartar.

The resultant alcohol, now almost completely free from water, will be our vegetable mercury; however it will require further refinements and administrations of our arte before it can be used. If we have collected the waters from the distillations and have kept them these will then be our phlegm and will be used later to help whiten our wine salts; whilst the remains of the red wine which will have darkened in colour is now gently evaporated in the flask. It is important that you do not use too much heat as we do not want to kill the vegetable life that it contains. This 'soup' will thicken to a tar-like consistency, which is referred to as 'the honey' and contains various salts and other empowering components such as the sal ammoniac which can be collected as a white salt as indicated by Hollandus' work on wine. This is a long process and will not be needed at this stage.

These salts are highly prized in the alchemical arte and as they come from the vine they are considered to be alive and therefore 'philosophical,' a term that is used in the arte to indicate that the subject in question is in an optimum state for the work to succeed. This is noted in the alchemical phrase, *'seek ye the salts that all men seek.'*

If we pour the distilled alcohol back over the honey and re-distil it, it will pick up these salts and other salts too. Another method would be to place an aludel on the flask; an aludel being a large flask with an opening at each end, the top opening will have a condenser or another aludel connected to it, which allows the alcohol vapours as they slowly rise to condense on the glass surface and run back down into the honey.

Thus, with gentle warmth a slow distillation takes place enriching the alcohol menstrum; this can be done for days and a week will suffice for our needs. The alcohol is now finally distilled off the honey which is now gathered from the flask, at this point as it is soaked in alcohol which of course is highly inflammable. This honey will need to be placed in a heatproof dish and calcined until it is a light colour, the lighter the better as this operation will burn off the dross.

When this is done place the hot ash into a flask which contains cold distilled water, be careful as this can splutter. Gently heat but do not boil this liquid; you will need to stir this mixture well as it will help to leach out the salts. After half an hour or so, you can let it stand and cool down. When the liquid is clear plug a glass funnel with cotton wool and pour off the clear water through it. The plug will filter out any debris and any un-dissolved ash. The clear water will need to be poured into a wide-bottomed dish such as a Pyrex dish, and gently heated. This will cause the water to evaporate and the salts to appear. These salts will be white, or of a white colour, which can be then recalcined, redissolved and evaporated again. By doing this the salts will become more clarified as they become more refined. It will also help to whiten the salts if they are washed with phlegm from the wine, but the phlegm will have to be redistilled before you use it for this operation.

Take these salts and place outside at night in a glass dish, they will mark the dish as they are corrosive so do not get them near any part of your anatomy that is sensitive, your eyes particularly as they will burn. If these salts are left exposed to the air they will deliquesce, that is, turn to water, as they suck the moisture out of the night air. This is important as this moisture will contain the secret fire, the prana, the chi or quite simply the life force of creation which is all around us. Dry the salts off and add to the distilled mercury and leave them somewhere warm to digest; this will allow the secret fire to 'set' in our mercury. After fourteen days distil the mercury off the salt and keep it in an airtight bottle somewhere dark, this will be our philosophical vegetable mercury and is much prized for our work.

It will be prudent to ferment your own wine for this work, although you can buy red wine to use. If you do not have a vineyard in the south of France (I wish) then you will have to either grow your own grapes for wine making which will be useful or quite simply buy 100% grape juice from the supermarket, juice that has had nothing added. Four one-litre cartons poured in a sterilized gallon demijohn with a few red grapes added and some wine yeast will in about 4-6 weeks give you sufficient red wine of about 10-11% alcohol to distil. After this time rack the wine off its sediment and let it clear; it will now be ready for the work.

Fixed Mercury of the Vegetable Kingdom

This is a menstrum that is made from red wine. Take red wine, if possible that we have fermented ourselves as it will then be alive, and add some organic red wine vinegar to it, leave it exposed to the air and somewhere warm, and in a few weeks time this wine will have transmuted into vinegar; this vinegar will contain our fixed mercury. This fixed mercury is then extracted by freezing the vinegar in plastic bottles that are two-thirds full. When the contents of the bottles have frozen, the vinegar spirit, because it freezes at a lower temperature than the water, will collect at the lowest point in the bottle and by tipping the bottle upside down can be made to run out and be collected.

Leave the contents of the bottle to thaw out and collect the coloured water; there will however still be some vinegar trapped in the ice. You will now have a flask of deep red concentrated vinegar and a bottle of ice which is the water. This water is the phlegm, which we will need, and should be placed to one side. Take the red vinegar, much reduced now in volume, but becoming highly concentrated, and re-freeze as before. Repeat the operation of letting it thaw out and collecting the concentrated vinegar as before. After this second freezing pour the vinegar into a retort and gently distil the water off, try not to let the water temperature go over 100°c as the vinegar will start to come over too. Reduce the liquid in the flask by a third and then change receiving flasks, gently increase the heat and the vinegar spirit will start to come over. Stop when the liquid begins to form a honey as in the wine distillation work. This is because you do not want to damage the sulphur of the vinegar which is in the colour.

The clear and concentrated vinegar spirit is now poured over the vinegar honey and either circulated via the aludel method or distilled off and poured back on when it has cooled down. This can be done several times to enrich the menstrum. By taking up the salts that are in the vinegar honey we are creating a suitable menstrum for a wide variety of works, both in the metallic and mineral kingdoms.

As before, take the honey out of the flask and calcine it, this will not be inflammable as it is not soaked in alcohol. These calcinations will be slow and take time and they will need to be done outside as they produce a lot of unpleasant fumes that will do you no good. When the ash has turned to a light grey colour, place it in a flask and cover it with the vinegar phlegm which we saved earlier. Heat gently but do not boil, then filter as was done with the wine salts. Now the liquid needs to be evaporated off and the salts collected. Repeat these operations, including the calcinations, but use distilled water this time for washing the salts. When these salts are white and pure place outside at night during a waxing moon and then gather them in before sunrise and dry them off gently. These salts are to be added to the vinegar spirit which is then placed somewhere dark and warm; this will allow the life energy to incubate within our menstrum thus preparing it for the higher workings of our arte.

The Sulphur....Both Fixed and Volatile

Place your plant material in a filter paper, (unbleached coffee filters are ideal) and place in a soxhlet which is attached to a flask which is half full of the extracting menstrum with a condenser connected to the top of the soxhlet. The flask is then heated to boiling point, no higher temperature is needed. The water evaporates and condenses against the cold insides of the condenser and then runs down into the soxhlet with the herbs that are placed therein. The chamber fills up with the menstrum and then overflows through the outlet tube at the top; and back into the lower heated flask. The liquid will again evaporate and condense as before thus repeating the operation. Two or three cycles of this work and the herb will have surrendered all its potencies. You will know when this has happened as the liquid in the soxhlet will become clear. If you change the herb and the filter paper the whole working can be repeated, this will create a strong herbal tincture very quickly; something which could take weeks is now produced in hours. The liquid will have a very fine oily layer on top which will in many cases be hardly perceptible, but this will depend on the herb in question as some plants are more generous than others at releasing their oils.

Better still, place the herb in a boiling flask and then half fill the flask with distilled water. Bottled water will suffice but distilled will be better, however do not use tap water for this work. Then connect a distillation head or bend to the flask which is then connected to a condenser and a receiving flask. As the water is heated it will bring over the oils which will condense and run out into the receiving flask. The water and the oil mixture must be decanted into a separating funnel from which the water can be drained off, leaving the oil behind.

If the oil is gently distilled it can be purified. Do not heat the oil too hot as we do not want to damage it and also be mindful that it is inflammable. This oil is the volatile sulphur; store it in a dark bottle, its perfume will be highly concentrated. However do not let the water in the flask with the herb dry out completely, therefore let it cool down before adding any more water to it, again half to two-thirds full will be ample as the herb will boil over which is not what we want to happen. Repeat this working a couple of times and then you will have retrieved most of the plant oils; the dark coloured water in the flask will contain many sulphur salts which are not volatile so they didn't come over with the oils. Therefore the water will need to be distilled off until a thick tar forms 'the honey'.

At this point, the mercury which is to be used in the work can be poured over this tar and distilled off. If this is done several times, then much of the plant's sal ammoniac and other salts will be absorbed by the mercury as previously mentioned. Afterwards pour out the tar mixture and calcine it. The salts are extracted as previously explained, and they can then be added to the salts which have been gathered from the calcined plant material. When this is done they should be added to the mercury which is now placed somewhere warm and dark for a lunar cycle. This allows it to digest and the alchemical secret fire to be set within the mercury. By doing so we will quicken the life therein and the life force which is in the atmosphere and is everywhere will manifest within our mercury; sometimes this can turn a pink colour and then you will know that it has truly set within the work.

Salt:

This is the plant's body and is produced by the calcinations of the plant material until it is a light gray ash. This ash is added to hot water and stirred, let it stand for several hours and then pour off and filter it through a funnel which has been plugged with cotton wool. As this drips through over many hours the impurities are left behind. This water, when it is evaporated, will release the pure salts of the plant which are its body. The black ash which will be left can be further calcined and the operation repeated a second time; this will produce further amounts of salt. The black ash which is then left over is the *'Terra Damnata'*, the damned earth, and is of no use to the working. These salts will need to be volatilised for the higher plant workings and the methods to do this have always been kept secret and only handed on to the student by the teacher. The volatilization of the salts is an important part of the work and because this is a major key which grants success to some alchemical workings of a higher nature, it is the reason why these methods have been kept secret. I am aware of five methods to perform this operation.

- The hot salt/cold oil combination; which I will explore in the rosemarius elixir.
- The circulation of the volatile mercury over the fixed salts.
- The maceration of the salts with the Fixed Mercury of the Vegetable Kingdom
- The circulation of the salts with aqua angelus.
- Finally the method of Philalethes; who after ten years of experimentation eventually found an important means of ingress into this Arcanum.

The volatilization of salts was an alchemical conundrum that the American alchemist George Starkey, who wrote as Ierenius Philalethes, explored during the 1650's after he had been reading extensively what the Belgium alchemist Van Helmont had written previously in his work *Ortus Medicinae*. In this work he commented upon a menstrum which he referred to as his Liquor Alkahest, a menstrum which could unlock the potency of all that was bathed in it. This was an alchemical 'cause célèbre' and was second to only the Philosophers' Stone in the great alchemical quests of that time. As Van Helmont's works were rather abstruse many who aspired to this 'Holy Grail' were left bereft of its powers.

Taking pity on these students of the arte, Van Helmont acknowledged that it was a difficult work and if it couldn't be achieved then he suggested that the alchemist should learn how to volatize salts, particularly wine tartar salt. He claimed that volatilized salts were able to perform some of the work of the Liquor Alkahest, but not all. Van Helmont wrote as such:

> *'...if you cannot attain this Arcanum of fire,*
> *learn then to make salt of tartar volatile*
> *and complete your dissolutions by means of it.'*

These alkaline salts are known to be cleansing and also corrosive; Van Helmont recommended them for the reduction and removal of bladder and kidney stones. However, according to science, plant salts and wine tartar salt, both of which are potassium carbonate cannot be made volatile, yet the alchemist would say that this is not so. If however these salts are heated to a red heat for hours nothing happens yet volatile salts when gently heated will quickly fly upwards and are extremely mobile. One method that Starkey discovered and which he wrote about in his notes was to take the plant salts of any plant that the alchemist was working with and combine them with the oils that had been distilled from the plant. Then more of the plant material is added to the mix and the resultant paste exposed to the air for several weeks without heat. Filter and gently distil off the liquids, and the salts that remain will be volatile and determined to the plant from which they have originated, that is they will be charged with the potency of the plant in question. Starkey also showed how to perform the volatilization by using oil of turpentine, also known as terebinth. With this the salts are mixed with the oil and left to digest again for several weeks and then the liquids are distilled off.

Writing in *Ortus Medicinae*, Van Helmont says that the salts are to be mixed with oil of cinnamon and the whole then converted into a volatile salt by an artificial and hidden circulation of three months; he also says that the salts must be free from water, therefore the salts must be heated first thus driving forth all moisture.

Writing in his notebooks Starkey says:

> '...I have learned that this mutation of oil into true salt
> can be performed by no art as successfully as it is done in the open air.
> And this is the 'hidden and artificial circulation' which is done by the fire of nature.'

Again in *Ortus Medicinae* Van Helmont declares:

> '...If the air (let him who can, grasp an Arcanum) first of all volatilizes the sulphur of a concrete with
> complete separation of its salt, this salt
> (which otherwise would be fixed by the fire into an alkali in the coal)
> will be made entirely volatile and will ascend sometimes in a liquid form
> and sometimes in the form of a sublimate.'

He goes on to say that by this means all the essential properties and virtues of the original body are preserved in the volatilized salt.

During March 1656 Starkey records that by creating a paste out of plant salts and oils which is then exposed to the air for several weeks until they unite, and then dissolving the mixture in an alcoholic solution which is then filtered and finally gently distilled off., the salts which are now left behind will be volatile and he referred to these as the 'Elixir of volatile salt.'

Aqua Angelus:

This method is quite a simple one: if the salts are left exposed to the night air during the waxing moon and kept out of sunlight during the daytime then they will eventually turn to water as they suck the moisture out of the air. The resultant mixture is gently poured into a distillation train or retort and distilled off. The water that comes over and is charged with the life forces that are present in the atmosphere is the Water of Angels, the Aqua Angelus. The dry salts are placed in a flask and the water is poured over them. If an aludel is fixed upon the flask this will give room for circulation and for the expansion of the contents, as it must now left somewhere warm to gently circulate. Then, after several weeks, if the water is distilled off, the salts will be volatile. As the water evaporates and condenses upon the cooler surface of the glassware it drips back down into the salts below. This gentle circulation and digestion will eventually cause the volatilising of the salts which will be seen as they creep up the walls of the flask.

Maceration of the Salts with the Fixed Mercury:

Again Van Helmont explains that if salts are dissolved in warm wine vinegar as we have previously prepared and then set to digest for forty days and nights they will become volatile. After this time the vinegar is distilled off the salts and the remaining salts are left behind as white crystals. Now they must be added to distilled rainwater and dissolved and the water distilled off the salts. Take the salts, place them in a sealed flask, and let them sit somewhere warm for a month. The salts will sublimate and fix to the walls of the flask; these are the volatilized salts.

Figure 14: The salt will quickly start to volatise if done as the arte demands

The Circulation of the Volatile Mercury and the Salt:

Our salt and the mercury (alcohol) do not mix and the mercury will float over the salts. Therefore we place our salt in a large flask or pelican and cover it with our mercury. We then leave it to circulate and digest for a week after which the mercury is distilled off and kept. The salts are now recalcined and when cool they are added to the mercury and the cycle of circulation and digestion is repeated. Afterwards our mercury is again distilled off and the salts are once more calcined. By repeating this operation several times the salts will become dough-like and volatile as they become more spiritualized.

Hot Salt/Cold Oil:

If hot dry salts are quickly poured into cold essential oil and then heated, the salts will volatilize very quickly. This working is the key to the work of the plant elixir and will be explored in more detail under the Rosmarius working.

CHAPTER FIVE

Aqua Opus: The Water Works

Water is the very stuff of life and our bodies are 90% water, so it is not surprising how we are affected by it, nor the subtle lunar currents which rule over the ebb and flow of the aqueous kingdoms. Traditionally water carries the life-giving currents that are expressed via the Eastern system of Feng Shui whereby the rain carries the energies of life from the heavens as it flows along the watercourses of the hills and valleys, meandering as it does, skirting hillsides. Sometimes being blocked and going stagnant, the life-force then becomes toxic psychic pools in the landscape where the inhabitants of the area do not flourish. On the other hand, where the flow is gentle and uninterrupted the inhabitants will prosper.

This energy can be captured and alchemically manipulated which will benefit the operator of the arte in various endeavours should they choose to do so. Not all water is the same: tap water particularly is to be avoided as are stagnant waters full of putrefaction. Water that has been caught in a thunderstorm is best, providing that it has not touched metal. Water from a brook or waterfall is also good, particularly where it runs over stones and bubbles and gurgles, singing the songs of the undines and water spirits. Also water that has been drawn from a holy well in the name and the blessing of the saint is most potent for the arte.

One can indeed collect dew before sunrise and this is good too. If you wish to proceed with this as your menstrum then you must wait until the sun appears in Aries, Taurus or Gemini as in these spring months the vitality in nature is at its strongest. To gather the dew a cloth such as a clean towel is pinned to a stick at each end and dragged over the surface of clean grass. Tie a string to the one end and simply walk in a straight line dragging the cloth; the stick at the back will weigh the material down and make it easier to drag this along the ground. Then when the cloth is soaked wring it out into a bucket. The waters will however contain various debris so the dew water must be filtered a couple of times to clean this matter from it. Another method of dew collection can be seen in the alchemical text *'Mutus Liber'* or the *'Dumb Book'* whereby a man and a woman are wringing out sheets which they have pegged to the ground. They are gathering the dew before it touches the ground because if it does then it is only suitable for works of the vegetable kingdom. Failing any of these methods, simply catch rainwater by leaving bowls and buckets outside during a downpour. Do not let the water come into contact with metal therefore use glass or plastic containers.

Collect a minimum of two litres for this work and place it in a plastic bucket which is covered to keep out dust and other foreign bodies. Pour some of the angel water which we explored earlier into the water and then put it somewhere dark and warm for several weeks. This water will undergo fermentation and will start to become viscous and sticky and needs to be periodically stirred with a stick. Do not touch it with your body at this stage. This is putrefaction whereby our arte declares that *'our work starts in darkness and in death.'* It is being reduced back to its primal state where it can be brought to a more refined state and its potency enhanced.

This water will be distilled into twelve fractions which will be the four elements, each of the elements then being separated into their mercury, sulphur and salt attributes. Shortly after the full moon and when the moon is travelling through a fire or an air sign half of the water must be distilled off. This water will contain the volatile aspects of our water which have come over first, these are the air and fire elements; that which is now left behind will be the fixed aspects which contain the earth and water elements of our water and these will be distilled accordingly. Wait until the moon is in a fire sign and take the distilled water and pour it into a flask and place an aludel on top of the flask to which has been attached a distillation head and train. The water is heated to 100°c and a slow distillation takes place which is collected in a receiving flask. Making the water travel higher to the outlet will ensure that only the most volatile parts come over. Stop when half of this water has come over. You will now have the fire aspects of the water which have now been distilled off and are in your receiving flask. That which is left in the distillation flask contains the air element. When the moon is domiciled in an air sign continue with the distillation, but leave 50ml or so in the bottom of the flask as the phlegm; this can be added to the undistilled water. Keep this air aspect which you have now distilled off sealed and safe. You now have the fire aspect as the most volatile and the air fraction as the volatile aspect of the water.

You also have the fixed aspects awaiting distillation: pour the 50ml of water left over from the air distillation into the water which contains the fixed aspects and has as yet not been distilled. This water is either now placed into a retort, or simply take off the aludel and attach the distillation head and train to the flask and then distil; this is done when the moon is travelling through a water sign. Stop when half of the liquid has distilled over, you now have the water element which you have collected in the receiving flask; the water which is left in the retort and has gone cloudy will be the earth element of the water. Therefore we now have the four elements which will need to be further subjected unto our arte.

Taking the water that is the fire element which we distilled over first, it is again distilled, this time into thirds. That which comes over first is the sulphur, the second third which is distilled off is the mercury, and the last third that comes over will be the salt. Collect these thirds and keep them in separate marked flasks; the sulphur will be associated with the astrological sign Aries as it is the most active, the mercury with Sagittarius as it is mutable and the salt will be considered to belong to Leo as the most fixed.

The air element of the water is also distilled in a like manner. The first third is the sulphur of the air aspect of the water and equates with Libra, the second third is the mercury of the air element and belongs to Gemini whilst the last third is the salt and is attributed to Aquarius.

Again the same is done for the water aspect, the first third of the sulphur is associated with Cancer, the second third, the mercury, belongs to Pisces and the last third, the salt, equates with Scorpio.

The earth aspect of the water is treated a little differently. The water is cloudy and contains a salt and an oil, when the moon is in an earth sign gently distil the water. The first third, that comes over first, is the sulphur which equates with Capricorn, the second third that distils off is the mercury, and this is associated with Virgo and will be oily. Dry off the rest and you will have a residue which is now to be calcined; the salts that are present will need to be extracted with distilled water as we have done elsewhere and these are of the nature of Taurus.

Once this is done, place the clean salts in a flask and add the water associated with Virgo and then add the water associated with Capricorn and distil both off; collecting the first half that comes over as belonging to Capricorn and the remaining water which comes over as being of Virgo. When everything has cooled down, repeat this operation twice more, as this will help to enrich the alchemical properties of this particular menstrum. On the last distillation leave a little of the water with the salt as this will be of the fixed nature of Taurus.

Element/attribute	Earth	Water	Fire	Air
Mercury	Virgo	Pisces	Sagittarius	Gemini
Sulphur	Capricorn	Cancer	Aries	Libra
Salt	Taurus	Scorpio	Leo	Aquarius

Figure 15: Astrological correspondences for the elements and attributes

These twelve waters have their own attributes, which are of the nature of the twelve signs of the zodiac and these are useful in the magics thereof. More importantly if the waters which are associated with the fire element are combined and then circulated in a pelican or by an aludel (or if neither are available place in a large flask and seal), their potencies will be increased. The container that they are in must be kept warm and needs to be left for a couple of days while the moon travels through a fire sign, then we will have created the elemental Archeus of Fire.

This process can be repeated for the three other remaining waters thus creating the Archeus of the other three elements. This work can be enhanced by prayers and invocations to the element concerned as this will help to connect with the relevant elemental current. These four Archeus' are useful when working with the four elements, such as in creating the elemental Condensers in Franz Bardon's work *'Initiation into Hermetics.'* Furthermore combine some of the four waters and you will have created the Universal Archeus of which a few drops can be imbibed as a general tonic. Also this water can be used in other magical works and tinctures; the alchemist is only limited by their imagination as it is now a good carrier of the magical current when it is charged according to arte.

CHAPTER SIX

The Seven Helpers: Seven Planetary Tinctures

The seven planetary tinctures are alchemical plant extractions which are used to assist the development of the alchemist. By taking them regularly the psyche becomes more attuned to the subtle currents of creation that are all around us and within which we have our being. The individual starts the course on the day of the week that they are born, thus if you were born on a Thursday then you would start on a Thursday. Starting with the tincture of Saturn they follow the Kabbalistic planetary order.

- Day 1 = Tincture of Saturn
- Day 2 = Tincture of Jupiter
- Day 3 = Tincture of Mars
- Day 4 = Tincture of Sun
- Day 5 = Tincture of Venus
- Day 6 = Tincture of Mercury
- Day 7 = Tincture of Luna

Ideally the alchemist will place a couple of drops of the planetary tincture in a glass of water and with the use of suitable planetary invocations will invoke the planet's energy and en-hallow the glass of water and then drink it as a living talisman which can be consumed.

If you are unable to do this in the planetary hour then perform this working upon rising in the morning. Of course this simple action will lend itself to the development of more complex planetary rites whereby the water will become a living sacrament. Such works will assist in the general use of planetary energies and their invocation or indeed their evocation.

Suggested herbs for each planet:

- Saturn....Horsetail
- Jupiter....Lime Flower
- Mars....Pepper
- Sun....Rosemary
- Venus....Rose
- Mercury....Fennel Seed
- Luna....Jasmine Flower

Other herbs can be used if any of the above are unavailable; for this I would suggest that you consult with Culpeper's herbal; which gives clear indications of each herb's planetary attributions. Culpeper was of course an astrologer as well as an herbalist and is a reliable source to consult.

Assuming that the alchemist is gathering the herb as opposed to buying the herb from a reputable herb supplier, it should be done on the planetary day and preferably during the first hour of the day which will belong to the planet in question. If not you will have to work with the next planetary hour. The alchemist asks God(s) for a blessing upon the work and invokes the energies of the planet involved and the spirit of the plant too. If all seems well, harvest the plant with a clean cut and leave an offering for the plant spirit; milk and honey are good or better still some water for the plant which has had a couple of drops of your blood added will be welcomed as a bond between you both. Do not let the plant touch the ground now that you have harvested it as the energies of the plant are dissipating the moment that it is cut and this will be quickened if it comes in contact with the soil again.

The fresh plant will contain more of the life force than the dried plant but this will not apply to seed or fruit as they contain the future potential of the plant itself. If you are using dried plants they are still acceptable but fresh is the ideal, although they may be unavailable depending on the time of year. Take the plant material into your laboratory and with 250ml of alcohol and 250ml of water place all together. Now again invoke the energy of the planet and the plant spirit to assist in this your operation of the arte.

Pour the water into a 1-litre flask and cut the plant material so that you can place it in an unbleached coffee filter, this is then placed in the soxhlet and is now connected to the flask. On top of this connect a condenser which has a stream of cold water running through it. The water for the condenser is provided from a bucket which has an aquarium pump pushing and recycling the cold water around the condenser, this is a far simpler solution than having the system connected to a running cold tap and wasting gallons of water every time that you use it.

We now heat the flask and this can be done via a heating mantle or a hot plate; if you are using a hotplate then embed the flask in a saucepan of sand which will provide a steady and even heat all around the flask. Heat the water in the flask so that the steam will rise through the soxhlet and condense upon the cold glass and run back into the herb in the soxhlet chamber.

When this is full of water it will run back down into the lower flask drawing with it the power and potency of the plant. Do this a couple of times until the plant material is exhausted. Then let it cool down and add the alcohol; our vegetable mercury. The alcohol is now heated at a lower temperature; just enough for the alcohol to evaporate as this will allow it too to make an extraction from the plant. Take the plant material outside and calcine in a saucepan. This can be done on a camping stove; any alcohol that is still in the plant will help to burn the plant material. Once it has stopped smoking place a lid upon the saucepan to stop any ash flying away, continue until the ash is a little grey in colour, then collect and keep. The flask with the herb extract is distilled off, not too harshly, as there will be the plant sulphur within the extract which we do not want to burn and destroy. When a ring starts to form around the inside of the flask we will have distilled off the components which we require, and we will then have a clear distillate in our receiving flask; keep this safe and sealed. The contents of the flask are gently evaporated until it thickens, this is the honey residue which will contain various alchemical compounds.

The clear distillate which has been distilled off and kept is now poured upon this honey. Either connect an aludel and circulate it for a few days or place the flask somewhere warm and dark for a month where it can quietly digest. Either way, at the end of its time it is distilled off again and is kept sealed. The residue is taken out of the flask and calcined until it is light grey, this may take some time to achieve. However do not use too violent a heat on the residue as any volatile salts present will quickly disappear. When you have calcined the matter to an ash this will contain the fixed sulphur salts...the sal sulphurous. These salts must be extracted from the ash; to do this we can place them into the grey ash from the calcined plant material that was produced earlier, as the plant ash will contain the sal salis... the salt of salts, the plant salts. Having mixed both ashes together place them in a soxhlet as was done previously with the plant material.

Extract the salts by using a menstrum of 95% distilled water and 5% distilled vinegar, and then gently evaporate the water. This will quickly extract the salts and help to whiten them. Repeat the operation on the ash twice more as this will draw out all of the salts from the ash. If you now evaporate the water, this will leave clean white salts behind in the dish. These salts can again be calcined and extracted again and they will be even purer.

On a waxing moon place the salts outside in the night air so that they can soak up the vitality in the atmosphere; bring them inside before the sun rises. These salts will be moist and after a few nights of this treatment they will be quite liquid. These salts and the water that has been captured by them can be added to the clear distillate, do this in the planetary hour of the plant. Seal the flask and place somewhere warm and dark for forty days and nights, to digest and marry; it will be useful to add a little gold to the tincture as this will help to hold the energies within the tincture, two drops of your blood will also work but if you do this then it is highly personalised and you do not want anyone coming into contact with it. If again it is consecrated to the planet in question or simply charged via meditation then you will have a useful ally in your works.

Pelicanization:

This is a little-used method that deserves to be more widely known as it follows the methods of nature, though it will only work with fresh herb material. In the wild when a plant breaks down the volatile aspects will evaporate whilst the non-volatile components will drop on the ground and rot; for the alchemist this is a formula that is easy to emulate.

Take the herb in question and quickly cut it finely and then pulp it with the mortar and pestle; some alchemists will use a food blender for this part of the work. However you do this you do not want to hang about as the plant material will be losing some of its vitality and the volatile parts will be already escaping. Place the material in a sterile jar and seal it well; this is important as we do not want to lose any more volatile aspects than we already have. This flask must be left to digest at an ideal temperature of 30°c for forty days and nights. During this time the fixed and volatile parts will start to separate from each other, and this will be seen as a liquid separating from the plant material. The liquid will contain some small amounts of alcohol which will carry the plant's life force with it and while it is in contact with the plant material it will also extract some of the oils that will be present.

This will not be a great amount as some plants will have more oils present than others and unless it is a very big jar that will hold kilos rather than grams do not expect to gather a large harvest. Therefore the liquid which eventually separates will contain some alcohol and the life force of the plant as well as some of the plant oils. Do not open the jar at this stage as we may lose some of the volatiles. After the forty days and nights place the jar in the fridge for twenty-four hours and let it settle. On the planetary hour relevant to the working open the jar and quickly pour off the liquids into a clean flask. Press the plant material to recover any further liquid, and store the liquid in a tightly sealed flask. However if the alchemist has performed this working in a flask rather than a jar they can gently distil all the liquid off the solids thus simply leaving the dry plant residue behind in the flask; the liquid part is to be stored as previously mentioned in a tightly sealed flask in the fridge. The plant material itself can now be calcined and the salts gathered as the arte demands. The volatile components are still to be separated further, remember this liquid will contain the mercury and the sulphur of the plant. Pour the contents of the flask into a retort or distillation train and gently distil off the liquid until there is only a resin left.

The liquid is now the mercury but it will have some of the volatile sulphur with it and the resin will contain the fixed sulphur salts. The resin is now scraped out and stored separately. Any that is left can be washed out with alcohol and the alcohol gently evaporated which will leave the sulphur behind in the dish. Now we have the mercury, the volatile sulphur combined with the mercury (the sulphur can be further separated from the mercury but it is likely to be only a few mls unless you have used a couple of kg of plant material; for the planetary tinctures it will suffice as given), the salt of the sulphur in the resin, and the plant salts from the calcined plant material, which we have freed and purified. These are never found free in nature as they are locked together in the expression of the plant's life.

Take the mercury which we have collected from our plant and add to it an equal amount of alcohol; this can be the alcohol which has been distilled earlier from red wine. Place them in a flask and seal tightly, and leave to digest for a couple of days. The resin is calcined and the salts are extracted, these salts are added to the plant salts. The salts are ground fine and are left outside at night during the waxing moon and treated as the other salts have been.

After seven days they are ready to add to our mercury and sulphur which we have waiting. Add these during the planetary times with invocations before and after invoking the goodwill of the planet to aid you in your workings. The flask which now contains the mercury, the sulphur and the salt is sealed and the contents left to marry somewhere warm and dark. It can be useful to stand the flask upon the relevant planetary square as this is considered to help concentrate the energies too. After forty days and nights bottle the tincture and it is then ready for use. It can of course, be en-hallowed further as mentioned earlier.

Via Hollandus:

Writing in his 17c work *Vegatabilis*, Hollandus offers the reader a way of working with plants that uses a dry distillation method. This is in some ways a follow-on way of working to the pelicanisation method given previously as they both use freshly cut plants. Hollandus' work produces a plant stone but I have adapted it to use creating our seven helpers, although there is no reason not to work as he instructs and create a stone of the vegetable kingdom. Having harvested your plant Hollandus says to remove all moisture as this is what is holding the plant back from allowing its powers to be accessed. To do this, place the plant in a flask out of sunlight, and heat gently not any more than 100°c or thereabouts, this will drive off the watery phlegm.

Some alchemists will take the plant material out of the flask at this stage and increase the heat. However as the moisture has come off the plant and some of the water will be in the flask with the plant I would suggest that you can simply turn up the heat sufficiently to drive any further moisture out of the plant and the flask so that it will distil over. Keep this water and change the receiving flasks. The plant material is now heated so that it starts to burn, this is dry distillation also known as pyrolytic distillation which is heat destructive and will break down the plant. Various substances and smoke will come over and condense in the receiving flask. Hollandus refers to this as our spirit which will contain the life forces. To do this keep increasing the heat every couple of hours, this slow increase will drive over different parts of the material.

The smoke which comes over, and which you are to collect, will come over at first as a white smoke, then with an increasing heat it will be red and finally yellow. Hollandus considers this to be the air element of the plant. After the white smoke has come over and you have increased the heat for a few hours, an oil will distil over; afterwards the plant is finally calcined for the salts that it contains. Now we have all the volatile components: the water which came over first, the coloured smoke as the air element which has condensed, the oil as the fire element and finally the calcined body from which you have purified the salts.

The spirit which came over as the coloured smoke can now be redistilled to purify it further; although this would be more relevant for higher workings such as a plant stone it is still useful to do this as various materials will have attached themselves to the spirit which we do not need. The oil will need to be gently redistilled before it is added to the plant spirit and the spirit can now be digested with an equal amount of alcohol. Place this somewhere warm for seven days so that it can digest quietly in the dark. Afterwards add the salts which have been prepared as our arte demands. The menstrum can be circulated gently in a pelican or simply left in a large sealed flask for a further week.

Perform any of these workings with the other planetary herbs and you will thus create the seven helpers.

CHAPTER SEVEN

The Elixir Workings: The Arte of Salt Volatilization

The elixirs are deep working, and, as Van Helmont makes clear, owing to their purification and spiritualization they can penetrate deep into the body, thus bringing the benefits of the herb that they are manifested from. All elixirs must have the salts volatilised to be effective and without this work of arte they will be ineffectual. Therefore this is an important key to our work. We have so far considered how to extract the salts, the sulphurs and the mercury from all plants and this working will bring their potency to a new level via the Chymical Wedding. If we heat the salts they will expand and if they are rapidly cooled they will contract and this fact is the key which will unlock their powers.

Therefore let us take 150ml of rosemary oil (although we can work with any plant for this), and pour it into a 500ml glass retort. We next take 30gms of rosemary salts, these salts are of both the fixed sulphur and the salts from the calcined plant which have been left outside under the waxing moon without rain falling on them. In the daytime they are put under cover out of sunlight as we have done before. Our salts are then dried off so that they are free from moisture and by placing some of the salts upon a teaspoon and heating the spoon with the salts on an open flame they quickly become very hot. They are now poured carefully into the cold oil in the flask and the opening is quickly stopped.

Figure 16: Rosemary distillation

Figure 17: Rosemary oil distilled

This will cause a mini-explosion in the flask; you will hear the salts fizz as they hit the cold oils, if this doesn't happen then you do not have the salts hot enough and the volatilisation will not work. When the salts hit the oil and shatter a great white cloud will fill the glass retort and the room will fill with the strong scent of the herb. This has prepared the salts for our work, and they are now opening their body and allowing the sulphur to enter therein and this will grant the salt wings so that it can now fly. Thus we are making the fixed volatile which can be seen with the alchemical imagery of two dragons which are forming a circle by biting each other's tails, as in the iconography of Ouroboros. The one dragon that is winged is seen at the top of the cycle whilst the lower dragon is not winged. The lower dragon without wings is the un-volatilised salts and the winged dragon the volatilised salt as it is now flying.

Figure 18: Volatile and Fixed Dragons

When the salt cloud has settled and stopped fizzing the next spoonful of salts can be heated and then added to the retort as before. If you are using less oil and salts for this work, they will need to be in the same ratio; that is the salts will need to be one part salt – five parts sulphur. If you are assuming that you can get all the salts, sulphurs and mercury from the plant in question this may not be easy, depending upon the plant that you are working with. Some plants, such as the mints, fennel, rosemary, thyme and sage are more generous with the sulphurs that they will yield. Other plants, particularly lemon balm and mugwort are low in oils, thus the sulphur which they yield will be minimal. However, it is possible to get around this by buying good quality plant oil and simply calcining a kilo or perhaps two of the herb that you are working with, after of course you have first extracted the fixed sulphur salts from them.

Therefore, to recap: take one or two kg of the herb in question and distil off the sulphur. This can now be gently redistilled to purify it further. Place it in an enclosed container and keep it; any oil that you are buying in can be added to it. If you are doing this let them both digest somewhere warm and dark for seven days before you use them. If however you haven't distilled off the sulphur and are going to use the oil which you have bought in, this obviously won't apply to you.

Figure 19: Mugwort

The herb (whether one has distilled the sulphur from it first or not) is now placed in a bucket to ferment for a week. The mercury that is birthed can gently be distilled off and rectified; although this is not necessary but if you do it, is to be kept sealed and safe. Whilst this is the ideal it is not absolutely necessary and the mercury created can be sacrificed when the liquid is evaporated.

The liquid is poured off and evaporated until it forms a tarry mass. Take an equal amount of alcohol to the amount of oil that you are planning to use in this work. If you have distilled any of the mercury you will need to include this in the amount of alcohol that you are using. The alcohol, our mercury, is added to the tarry mass and is then distilled off; this is done several times and when complete must be kept well-stoppered.

All the tarry liquid is now calcined and the salts of the sulphur are now extracted from it, the plant material is also calcined and their salts are also to be extracted. Therefore we now have both the salts, which are combined, and the sulphur and the mercury too.

Figure 20: Distillation of mugwort

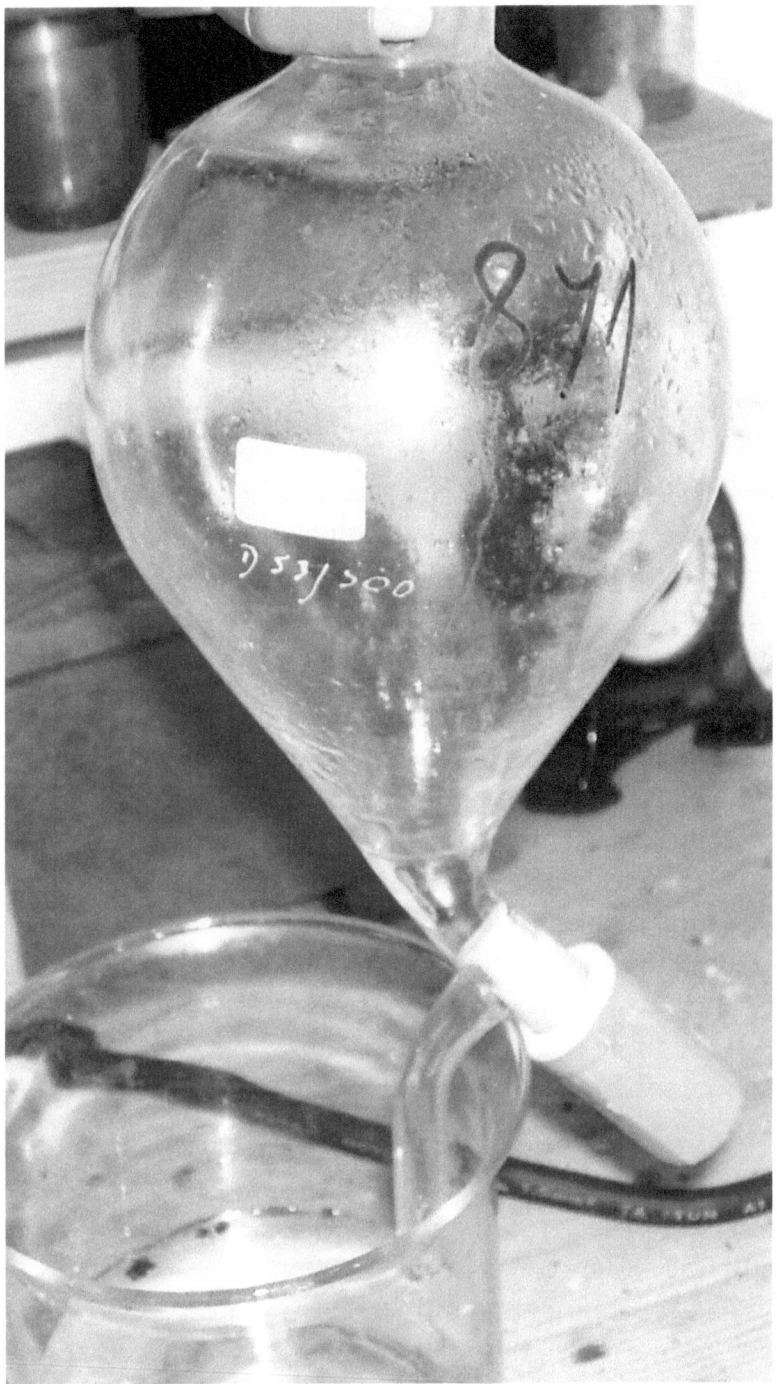

Figure 21: Oil of mugwort

Once the salts in the retort have settled down and stopped fizzing, the flask is heated just enough to distil the oils over gently, this will be about 250°c. Do not go much higher than this temperature as the sulphurs will burn and they will then lose some of their alchemical properties.

As the sulphurs start to distil, you will notice that there appears to be a snow storm happening in the retort as the volatile salts are now starting to fly upwards. It will look like the salts are falling as snow from the top of the flask, this is good as they are now considered to have gone heavenwards and are descending back to earth as spiritualized beings. As the sulphurs are distilling over you will begin to see a slight frosting in the beak of the retort; these are some of the volatilized salts and this is a good sign. Some of the salts will also come over in the oil, which you are collecting in a flask.

When you have distilled the sulphur over, leave the retort to cool down, and when it has done so you then pour back over the salts the sulphurs which you have just distilled off. Again you gently heat the retort and distil the sulphur back over into the receiving flask. This will cause more of the salts to volatize and will produce further frosting in the beak of the retort. This operation is done three times and will produce our sulphur which is now saturated with volatized salts.

Afterwards clean out the oily tarry mass in the bottom of the retort, but leave the salts which have frosted in the beak. Pour back into this clean flask the sulphur which you have distilled off three times and to it add an equal amount of the mercury which was prepared earlier. Now distil them both over together and they will appear in the receiving flask now married and conjoined. As the alcohol comes over it will wash any of the salts off the wall of the retort and they will all bind together in the alchemical marriage in our receiving flask. The salts which are the body will not marry to the mercury which is the spirit unless the sulphur, the soul of the plant, is present. Thus the three become one as the sulphur, the Red Man or King is married to the mercury, the White Woman or Queen; the white salts are the bridal gown. The elixir is now gently circulated and digested as the marriage is consummated and the alchemical child is birthed.

Figure 22: The Red Man and the White Queen

CHAPTER EIGHT

Vini Tartarus: Wine Tartar and its mystery

Wine tartar is a mysterious substance which is created by wine and holds many virtues. It is a crystalline substance which is found at the bottom of the wine tun after the fermented wine has been racked of its sediment and stood in a barrel to settle and clear. When the weather is cold the tartrates will precipitate more readily therefore late winter/early spring will be a good time to collect them. However the best tartrate will come from red wine which has been standing in an oak barrel. As modern winemaking tends to use stainless steel, oak wine butts are hard to find. There some vineyards in the UK and the acquisition of wine tartar, or wine stones as it is also known, is not too difficult. Perhaps surprisingly, vineyards are on the increase in the UK and can be found even in Wales; not an area noted for viticulture. Traditionally, within the alchemical world, wine stone has been considered potent in the production of various magisteries which will help alleviate what alchemy refers to as tartaric diseases, those whose nature is cold and fixed; such as arthritis, gout, rheumatics, stones and obstructions that are deep within the body.

Van Helmont suggests that wine stones can deeply penetrate the body and act on various levels to promote good health. The tincture of tartar has been considered to be good for a general cleansing of the body and can be used as a medicine to help purify the corpus. The traditional dosage has been a couple of drops in wine or water twice a day, sometimes for several weeks as its potency is unleashed. The wine stone is a key substance in the alchemical world as it is viewed as something which is both vegetable and mineral and therefore has a presence in both kingdoms. It is also of importance in working with antimony and in particular the production of the Antimony Regulus, or the 'Star of Basil' and in the confection of the Tartar Alkahest which will grant access to the sulphur of the metallic realms and the potencies thereof. It will also revivify 'dead metals'. Finally, a philosophical sal ammoniac will collect in the distillation train and will also be present in the alkahest which will allow it to work in the metallic kingdoms.

Firstly the tartar must be crushed and reduced to the size of a pea, however do not powder the tartar as it will clog the glassware, but neither should it be used in big chunks. Place it in a flask and tilt the flask on its side so that the neck is horizontal this will help the volatile extracts to come over more easily as they are heavy in nature and will not rise up so readily. The distillation train is a little more complex, as illustrations show, as it needs to be airtight but also allow for an escape of pressure should it build up.

Firstly the temperature is gently increased and eventually watery phlegm will pass over into the first receiving flask which then will stop. When this happens, quickly change the first receiving flask and make sure all joints are still airtight. Place ice around the first and second receiving flasks as this will help the distillate to condense. The heat is increased slowly, and a white smoke will rise from the tartar; this is the rising of the spirit and it is now that the oil and the alkahest will also arise. The oil comes over now as a red-black stinking oil and is unpleasant, whilst it is considered to be carcinogenic it also has healing properties. This is because it promotes rapid cell growth which can get out of control; the oil will float on the condensed liquid which collects in the flask from which it can be skimmed off.

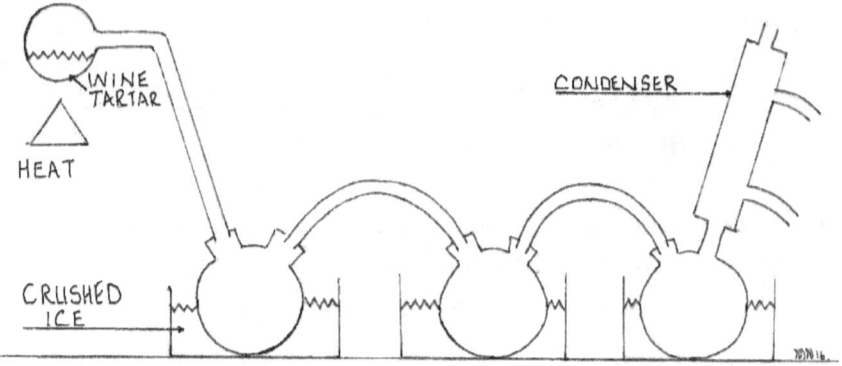

Figure 23: Tartar distillation train

The pale yellow distillate which will condense in the receiving flasks contains the alkahest and this will need to be kept cold. A new distillation train is set up and the receiving flask will need to be embedded in crushed ice as this will help to condense the vapours which will distil over. As the distillate comes over it will split into two components. One a clear liquid which will be the alkahest and secondly a light yellow oil; this will be the sulphur of tartar. It does not stink as does the black oil which came over in the first distillation and this non-toxic oil is considered to be something of a 'heal all.'

However the difficult part of this second distillation is that the receiving flask is to be exchanged once the first part of the distillate has come over; this needs to be done quickly and with some skill as the alkahest will quickly evaporate. It can be stored in a sealed flask and kept cold; it will revive alchemically dead metals and also extract their sulphurs.

We now have the alkahest, the light yellow oil of tartar, the stinking oil of tartar and the tartar residue still in the flask; although the flask may well have broken with the increased heat which will be needed to push the volatile substances over. If the flask is slowly allowed to cool it can sometimes be saved. The remnants of the tartar are now to be calcined, but firstly they are to be ground fine with the aid of a mortar and pestle as this will help with whitening. Calcining tartar is a slow process and will take some time which cannot be rushed; therefore patience is the key. When they are reduced to a light grey colour they can be dissolved in distilled water and evaporated to regain the salts. As with previous work, this operation of calcining and leaching the salts can be repeated and their purity will increase.

The salts are the Sal Tartari and within them is hidden a blue salt which has the real potency of this kingdom. To access this salt the white tartar salts are placed in a crucible with a lid and calcined, this time at a temperature of 850-900°c. At this temperature they will melt; let them calcine for an hour, and then let them gently cool down. The lid will capture most of the volatilizing salts, so hopefully you will not lose too many of them; the salts in the crucible will turn a blue colour often the shade of a blackbird's egg. These salts are deeply penetrating, be it in the metallic or animal kingdoms, and as Van Helmont claims they take the medicine deep within the body tissue. The salts are ground very fine and left outside overnight as we have treated previously. In the morning they are dried off gently and placed in a round bottom flask. Onto these salts we now add a little of the light yellow oil and some of the alkahest which we have kept cold and sealed. To this we now add an equal amount of alcohol; as this is from wine, as is the tartar, they will combine readily. Place an aludel on top of the flask or simply place the ingredients in a big sealed flask and keep warm for a lunar cycle. This will allow for circulation to take place and will help to further to increase the potency.

Keep some of the salts back, as this portion will not need to be calcined at such a high temperature to bring out the blue of the inner sulphur, as these salts can be used in other alchemical works such as pouring alcohol upon them at a 40:60 ratio to absorb water; thus producing a very dry alcohol with practically no water in it. These salts can also be used to collect and distil the angel water as they readily deliquesce; finally, they are also used in antimony works such as the 'Star of Basil.'

Figure 24: Wine stone

CHAPTER NINE

The Primum Ens: Accessing the Essentials of Plants

Writing in his biography of Paracelsus, Franz Hartmann discusses the Primum Ens Melissa which is created from Lemon Balm. This, he makes quite clear, has the virtue to rejuvenate the body and lift energy levels to new heights. This is a fact that is also made very clear in Rubaphilos Salflure's work *The Hermes Paradigm Vol II* where he talks quite candidly about the effects that the Primum Ens had upon a friend of his. However in my own experience the Ens has always increased energy levels in all people who have ingested it, and also sexual appetites can increase as do levels of happiness... whether both subjects are inter-related is another matter, but general wellbeing will certainly improve. The effects of the Ens will be more pronounced upon older persons as the energy levels and life force of a young person are already at optimum levels.

It is also possible to create planetary Ens using the following techniques for workings with planetary spirits and their energies, which in itself will grant initiation into these realms. This can be done by using plants that resonate with any of the seven planets. However the Ens itself is not a physical subject but is something which can be 'accessed' as it takes up residency in a physical body. Such thinking is an important part of the alchemical corpus which is often overlooked, which then creates a scenario of treating alchemy as little more than an act of chemistry.

Technique:

Firstly we must use potassium carbonate to produce a lye for the work, this can be acquired via a chemical supply house. If you do this, then the 'pot carb' must be roasted for an hour, dissolved in distilled rainwater and gently evaporated to regain the salts. It can then be used for this work; also one can use the salt from wine tartar which we have previously worked with, or we can use the salts extracted from calcined vine prunings which are the preferred option to use where possible. The salts are left outside in a glass dish overnight and brought inside before sunrise.

You may have to do this for several nights as the salts will turn into a liquid which is very caustic so do not get it near any sensitive areas of your body such as your eyes for example, as it will burn. The optimum time to do this is in the months of March, April or May during a waxing moon. The resultant liquid is known as Oleum Tartari...that is Oil of Tartar. The oil of tartar is cleaned of anything which has fallen in it and any salts poured off that may remain; we do not want these as they will have an adverse effect upon the Ens that we are creating. The oil is placed in a flask and sealed, however owing to the caustic nature of the oil it will mark the glassware as it etches into the surface.

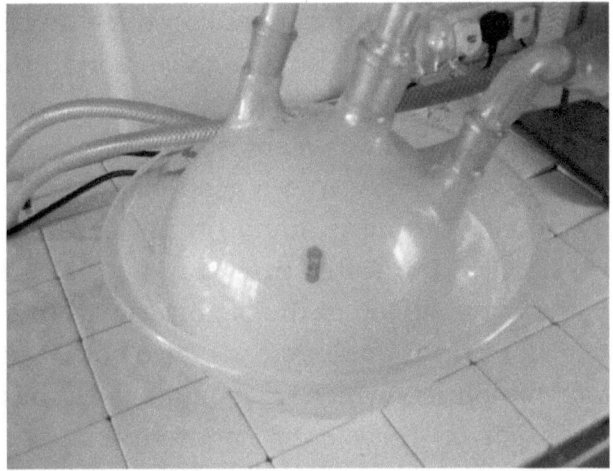

Figure 25: The stinking red oil of tartar

On the day and hour of Jupiter, and after following due protocol, the alchemist harvests a handful of lemon balm leaves which are then reduced quickly to a pulp; this can be done in a liquidizer which will produce a very finely cut herb. However do not waste time as the vitality of the plant will be evaporating and we do not want to lose this. The leaves must be freshly picked for this operation of the arte and not dried. When the leaves are added to the oleum tartari, we must also add a little more dry pot carb to counteract any moisture from the fresh leaves. Seal the flask and place somewhere dark and warm for twenty-four hours, no longer than forty-eight hours as we do not want too much of the plant sulphurs to be extracted in this work.

Traditionally the liquid is filtered off the plant material but the problem now becomes that some of the Ens is lost as it attaches to the plant material because it is now floating upon the surface of the oleum. The artist can instead pick the leaves out of the flask, shake a little, and try to dislodge any Ens that has attached itself to the material and hopefully thereby reduce any losses. However I have with success also moved on to the next stage of the work and simply left the plant material in the oleum and poured our mercury over the material to the depth of two fingers; it is a good idea to dry off the mercury first by letting it stand on pot carb for a few hours to absorb any water that may be present in it. This will float on the top of the oleum, whilst this is not ideal it does work, though you will also collect some of the plant sulphurs which can mar the work. The mercury is left on the oleum for twenty-four to forty-eight hours; it now becomes an emerald-green colour as it absorbs the Ens. In my experience with this work, often at this point, if the mercury is decanted off the oleum by using a pipette, (which will limit any loss of our material), the Ens becomes a shining deep green.

If a test tube containing some of the Ens is held up to a strong light this green is very pronounced, but if you then look at it from a different angle with the light shining through it you will see it as a deep maroon purple. Indeed if two people are looking at it at the same time and with the same light but from different angles both will see different colours as I have described. The Ens is to be gently distilled so that two-thirds of the mercury is evaporated; if this is collected it can be re-added to the oleum mix so as to absorb more of the Ens material and re-distilled, thus we will produce a highly concentrated product. The Ens is to be taken as ten drops in water or wine daily for two weeks and effects are to be noted upon the body and one's dreams.

Herbs for planetary Ens:

- Sun...rosemary
- Luna...mugwort
- Mars...nettle

- Mercury...lavender
- Jupiter...lemon balm
- Venus...rose
- Saturn...horsetail

CHAPTER TEN

Lapis Vegetabilis and the Circulatum Minor: Of the Vegetable Stone both Liquid and Solid

Plant stones are useful allies and the liquid stone, the circulatum, is not an easy work. Whilst there is much that has been published in the alchemical world, even by those that have achieved the circulatum, there has been no real and useful published account so far which will grant you success. I like to think I'm wrong, however nothing so far has convinced me otherwise. The solid stone is an easier work to confect but it is not the 'Philosopher's Stone,' so do not confuse the two works as they are different. The plant stone will grant access to the properties of plants, by placing the plant material in a flask of distilled water and leaving the stone in the water, this will cause the oils and the plant's mercury to float on the top, from where they can be collected. The stone when correctly made will not dissolve in the liquid.

The stone will also contain much of the power of the plant from which it has been made, thus if a few grains of the stone is digested, the plant's realm and the planetary aspects thereof can be ingressed. The Circulatum Minor however will also allow access to the plant's potentials too. The C.M. is a liquid in which plant material can be placed after which the sulphurs and mercuries will rise to the top and from which they can be collected, it will also work on amber and coral too; this menstrum if stored adequately can be reused. Both the C.M. and the stone are highly evolved alchemical products and will need to be kept away from the profane as much as possible, a stone for each of the seven planets can be produced and these will grant ingress into deep planetary levels thus promoting an initiation into the planets' mysteries.

Plant Stone:

Whilst it is possible to use plant oils already distilled and dried plant material, I am, for this account, using the whole plant material and approaching the work via the long path; although there are shortcuts which can be applied. If you are using seeds such as caraway or fennel, for example, then these will contain vital life forces which will aid the work. If you are working with dried plant material, such as rosemary or whatever is at hand and if it is not too old, it will still contain some of the plant's energies; however fresh plants are best.

You will need 4-5 kg of plant material for this work, but if you are using seeds such as the above and which are rich in sulphurs, 3-4kg will suffice; but this will depend upon how rich they are in alchemical materials. Ideally the herb material is to be cut in the planetary hour at the full moon when the plant's energies are peaking. Having taken note of Basil Valentine's wise words we make prayers and invocations to our God(s) for a blessing upon the work and that the plant's spirit will aid our holy undertaking. Pour an offering on the ground before the plant; water with a drop of one's blood added is good, as is milk and honey. After tracing the planetary symbols in the air over the plant, and with a suitable invocation, the plant is harvested; providing all seems well. Take note of the general vibe and omens prior to harvesting the plant, and do not let the material touch the ground after you have harvested it, as this will allow a leak of the plant's energies which will be looking to return to the earth so that they can dissipate. The offering will help to alleviate any hostility between the plant spirit and yourself, it will also help focus your will upon the work in question.

We are trying to develop empathy between the alchemist and the subject which is being worked upon, and this approach is always profitable concerning any alchemical workings that you are engaged upon. Thus the observed and the observer are having a subtle effect upon each other and through this intimacy a bond will form between the alchemist and the sacred child of their will. As the work is a mirror of the heavens we must also take note of the planetary circumambulations through the heavens. Thus the work is prepared at the full moon, regardless whether you have harvested the plant yourself or have bought it in from a reputable source. As the moon starts to wane we start the distillation of the plant sulphurs; of course if you have acquired the oils from a supplier of herb oil this stage will not apply although it would be a good idea and in keeping with our arte to gently distil the oil and treat it as if you have just distilled it of the herb.

Our arte, as the 'Old Masters' would say, starts in darkness and death; thus having distilled off the sulphurs as explained earlier we place the material in a receptacle to ferment with 0.5 kg of sugar and a little wine yeast. Brewing sugar from a homebrew supplier will be ideal as this will increase the mercury yield considerably. Within a few days or so the yeasts will have done their work and the liquor can be poured off the plant material which itself can be squeezed dry. The solids are to be calcined and the salts that are leeched from them as our arte demands are to be collected and saved. Let the calcinations take place when the moon is domiciled in a fire sign and as we are breaking down the plant material let it be when the moon is waning. We can also as the moon travels through an air sign distil off the mercury from the liquid. Let the mercury be rectified and dried off, that is made free as possible from any water which we do not want in the work; and it should now be kept in an airtight container. The dark waters that are left over are to be gently simmered and allowed to thicken and when they are at a honey-like consistency the mercury is poured back over them and distilled off. This is done several times which will greatly enrich the mercury with sal ammoniac, the alchemical salt, which will open the door to much of the alchemical kingdom.

This distillation and enrichment of the mercury is to be done as the moon waxes and when Luna is travelling through an air sign. The honey-like tar is now calcined and as it has been soaked in our mercury will quickly catch fire and this will whiten the ash far quicker than just plain calcinations without the mercury having been circulated or repeatedly distilled off. This white ash will produce the sal sulphuris...the salt of sulphur. Therefore we now have our mercury enriched and rectified, the volatile sulphur and the two salts, the sal sulphuris and our plant salts...sal salis. The two salts are to be combined and for forty days and nights they are to be left somewhere dark and out of the way, but exposed to the atmosphere. During this time as they are exposed to the air they will deliquesce and turn to liquid this will help them to become volatile. After this period dry them off gently and on the approach to the full moon leave them exposed to the beams thereof out in the open air. By leaving the salts exposed they are charged with our secret fire and thus become suitable for our work.

Our salts are now calcined at a high temperature and this will not be easy as temperatures of 900°c are needed. The crucible will need a lid on it to stop the more volatile salts from flying away. At these temperatures they will become liquid and furious, they will eat into the crucible and the lid may crack too. Pour the liquid salts into a hot crucible although not as hot as the one that they are in. You must exercise great care; goggles are a must as is protective clothing for any accidents may scar you for life. The salts when they are cool can be scraped out of the crucible; however this will not be easy as they will have vitrified. However if some of our mercury is poured on top and the salts are allowed to bathe in it for a few days much of the salt can be scraped out and will be dough-like in appearance.

These salts are dried off and placed in a small dark jar, during the planetary hour and day which governs them and on a waxing moon, they can be gently fed with a few drops of their sulphur which you have already gathered. Stand the jar with the salts in upon a planetary square relevant to the working, (these can be found in Agrippa among other sources)... thus if this is a work using rosemary, which is a plant of the sun, the sun square is used, likewise invocations and words of power which appertain unto this planetary work. Do not feed the salts with any more sulphur than they can absorb at any one time, a few drops will be plenty. The following month repeat the calcinations that you performed previously and gently pour the molten salts into a clean warm crucible as before. Again repeat the digesting with the mercury and the subsequent collecting of the salts. The salt will start to change in texture and appearance as it starts to become more pliable. The salts are again dried off and as previously are to be fed again with their sulphur and left to digest for a month. The operation is repeated a third time and the salt will become quite soft and malleable.

This can be repeated again, however your salt may be diminishing by now if you did not have much to start with. We repeat the work by feeding our stone, this time with our mercury, again just a few drops as it must not be swimming in the liquid. Let the salts be fed again with our mercury and left to digest somewhere warm and dark. After the third month, which will be the sixth, if we count the months imbibing our stone with its sulphur, we now re-calcine the stone and pour it into the hot crucible and leave to cool. It will be like a glass stone; to get it out of the crucible you may need to break the container, but very gently. The stone is to be rubbed with its sulphur regularly as this will help it to keep it waterproof and fed.

This stone is considered to be alive, an entity that has been birthed from the plant kingdom to which it belongs and has the potencies thereof. These can be re-enforced by the use of conjurations, meditations and other ritual practice. It is a disciplined and demanding work and a test of the alchemist's skills.

The Circulatum... The Liquid Stone

Whilst in many ways this work shares much of the praxis of the previous stone, it is however a very different creature and is more difficult to manifest. Whilst the modus of purifying the salt, sulphur and mercury is the same, the marriage of the tria prima is different. Much has been written about this work and Baron Urbigirus writing in the 17c has much to say which you may find useful. The same can be considered of Professor Junius's work, *'Spagyrics,'* however both writers leave out important parts of the process which leaves their work incomplete, but nonetheless useful and worthy of further study.

Firstly our mercury must be circulated over sal ammoniac and this must be philosophical. This can be produced by simply buying ammonium chlorate salts and soaking them in urine for a month. If the urine is distilled off (and this will stink), you will be left with the salts. These salts are heated within a dish that has a lid on; as the salts will now vapourise and collect on the cooler surface of the lid they can be scraped off from here. This is sublimation of the sal ammoniac and the most volatile parts will be collected for our use. They can now be re-heated and again the more volatile will sublimate, these will be the most volatile portion of the salts and fit for our arte. The mercury can also be circulated, as previously considered, over the honey which of course will enrich it considerably. The circulation must proceed for forty days and nights...our philosophical month. This mercury must be free from all water as far as possible and must be as much as 98-99% pure, which is a high concentration which will require skill to achieve. Our sulphur will need to be equal in weight to our salt and both must be pure and clean. The sulphur is poured into the flask and mixed with either a little of the honey-like tar that has been left from the distillation of the mercury or we can use Copaiba Balm which has a reputation for working well within this work. However if you do use Copaiba it must be re-distilled prior to use, either way, the idea of using Copaiba or the honey tar is that they will help to open the pores of the salt which is essential for the work to succeed; because the salt will have to be volatilized for success in this operation of the arte to occur.

The salt, which can be salt from wine tartar, is firstly left exposed to the air. This is done under cover and after several weeks it will have become very liquid due to its deliquescent powers; the salt is now dried off very gently as these salts have become quite volatile. At this stage add sal ammoniac at 10% of the salt's weight to the sulphur, the salts are now heated on a metal spoon so that they become very hot and will start to 'pop,' this is the time to spoon them into the flask which contains your oil/copaiba or honey tar mix. Quickly shut the flask as a cloud of volatilising salts will arise, and you do not want to lose any of them.

When the salts in the flask have settled they must be stirred gently and further hot salts are then poured into the flask which is again sealed. The flask is digested at 40°c and the sulphur/salt mixture must be stirred with a clean rod several times a day. After forty days and nights the sulphur-salt mix is removed from the warmth. Now we add our mercury which needs to be 10 times the amount of our sulphur and salt. The mercury is gently distilled off this and when everything has cooled down we then add the mercury back onto the sulphur and salt mix. The mercury is again distilled off and again it is repeated; this is done for as much as twenty cycles of distillation and cooling. The C.M. should have a sharp taste and a plant that is placed therein will separate into its three essential parts within a short time and the sulphurs and mercury will float on the top where they can be accessed; this will also work on amber and coral too. The C.M. can be reused and this will help with increasing its power.

CHAPTER ELEVEN

The Bhasma: Metals as Medicine

That metals can be used within a medicinal setting should come as no surprise and the alchemical arte has several methods that will grant ingress into this kingdom. One such path is the creating of Bhasma, an Indian form of alchemical practice. With this work a metal can be made sensitive to the body sufficiently so that its medicinal virtues are made accessible. With this in mind Zinc (Zn) is a good and useful metal to work with as it is useful in stimulating the immune system against many bodily foes.

Heat on a steel spoon small amounts of Zn, this can be powdered Zn and when the metal has melted pour it into a container that has a mixture of milk and yogurt therein; be mindful as it splatters. The Zn is now removed, washed and the heating and cooling in the mixture is repeated a further six times. When the Zn has cooled down reheat and add some yellow turmeric to the metal and continue to heat. If the contents of the spoon start to flame move the spoon a little higher from the heat source; you may have to play with this a little as we do not want the mixture to oxidise which will be indicated by the edges of the mix turning white; this will happen with too much heat. Add more turmeric and continue to heat, the mixture will stay black in colour.

Remove any metal that has not fused with the turmeric and do not let the mix fuse into a solid mass.

The black mass is now placed into a dish and more turmeric is added as is distilled water; a paste is thus made. This paste is placed into a crucible with a lid and heated at a much higher temperature; 750°c is the optimum temperature for this working which should last for three hours. After this allow it to cool down and add more turmeric to the mixture and reheat again at the previous temperature. This heating at a high temperature must be repeated twenty even thirty times before the Zinc Bhasma can be used, this can be done by adding a couple of grains, no more, to water and then consumed. Such workings, whilst simple, are very time-consuming, as can be seen with the constant calcinations; however this will awaken the healing properties held within the metal and grant access thereto.

CHAPTER TWELVE

Gemstones: The tinctures thereof

Gemstones have always been held in high esteem for their healing properties and with the alchemical artes the potency of gemstones can be accessed by the use of a menstrum such as an alkahest. This will release the potencies of the gemstone at a far higher level than a gemstone tincture would do; although a simple gemstone tincture would be improved by the circulation process. However our alkahest will release the sulphur of the gemstone in a short time and this oil can be ingested in very small doses in a glass of water to benefit from the gemstone potency, either magically or medicinally. However do not use malachite or stones bearing lead, for this we will use rose quartz.

Our alkahest for this work is created from the juice of the grape; therefore take 5 litres of red wine and 5 litres of red wine vinegar. The vinegar will need to be a live vinegar and not pasteurised as this will have killed off the alchemical life therein which we will need for the working; therefore homemade vinegar will be ideal as it will be alive. Pour the red wine vinegar into several plastic bottles and freeze it to extract the spirit which we have done previously and gently distil. The water comes over first, leaving the vinegar spirit behind as the spirit needs a slightly higher temperature to distil over, gently dry the remains until they become as thick as honey and then circulate the vinegar spirit over this for a few days, which will allow it to absorb various attributes which will aid in granting success in the arte.

The honey-like tar is now calcined and the salts extracted as we have done elsewhere, keep these dry and safe. The alcohol is distilled from the red wine and rectified; this will produce a strong mercury. As with the vinegar, the red wine remains must be gently dried to a honey-like consistency and the alcohol circulated over this for a few days too; after which the honey is calcined and the salts extracted. Both salts are mixed and ground together, after which they are left out all night under the waxing moon and retrieved before sunrise. These salts will need to be volatile which can be helped by leaving them exposed to the atmosphere somewhere dark and safe.

After a month gently dry them off and place in a circulation with the mercury; or add the mercury and distil off the salts which can then be dried and re-calcined, exposed to the air, and dried again. Then pour the mercury back over and re-distil. This operation can be performed several times as the salts and the mercury will become suitable for the work. After several distillations or days of circulation, add the vinegar spirit and distil all of the liquid over into a receiving flask which must have some alcohol therein with the beak of the retort therein so we do not lose any of the potency that comes over.

We now take everything that is left over from the distillations and any phlegm and the water from the thawed-out ice and calcine these with any solids from the retort; extract any salt that is present and add to the mercury. Pour into a retort an equal amount of the mercury and the vinegar spirit (our fixed mercury), and gently distil them both over into a receiving flask, the beak of the retort will need to be submerged in some alcohol to reduce the loss of any of the spirit as the bodies unite together. At the new moon circulate our menstrum between sunrise and sunset, let it cool down during the dark hours of night, then re-circulate at sunrise. This regime is continued until the full moon; when it is filtered and stored safely.

Having prepared the alkahest for the work we prepare the gemstone; this is done by fire. However it is firstly wrapped in an old towel and hit with a hammer, thus initiating the 'solve' process. When it is fractured it is heated in a crucible with a lid by placing it in a hot fire, 600°c would be the ideal; certainly the fire does need to be hot. It is then dropped into a bucket of cold water, and when cool is then reheated and the operation repeated several times taking care as it will spit and splutter as it rapidly cools down and starts to break into smaller pieces. The gemstone is then taken out of the cold water and needs to be ground very fine, when this has been done the ground stone is gently heated at 100°c for three days; as this will reduce any toxins that may be present.

After this procedure the gemstone is ready for extraction. During the planetary day and hour that governs it, and with suitable invocations of the energies involved, place the gemstone in a flask and pour the alkahest over it. The flask is then sealed and placed somewhere dark and warm to digest for forty days and nights. The flask is then placed somewhere cold and left to settle for fourteen days and nights.

The menstrum will be coloured according to the work in hand. It is now filtered and gently distilled. The beak of the retort is placed in the receiving flask and the flask kept cold in an ice bath or in very cold water, as this will discourage the loss of the spirit as it comes over. The oil will be left in the retort and is the soul of the gemstone and contains its healing and magical properties. This is to be stored in a dark bottle and kept dark and cool; one drop placed in a glass of water and drunk will release its potencies. When imbibing, it is useful to intone a suitable invocation for the working, indeed the gemstone sulphur can easily be charged with meditative and ritual practices. The alkahest which you have distilled off can be used again for further workings if it is kept safe.

CHAPTER THIRTEEN

Glauber and the Aurum Potable: The Medicine of the Sun

Gold contains great healing and magical powers which are not easily accessed; the 'King's Palace' is well guarded and does not yield its secrets willingly. Gold can be highly explosive in the right environment such as coming into contact with ammonia solutions, particularly when it is then heated, and you will need to remember this when working with the Red Man.

There are several methods to gain ingress into the 'King's Palace' and we will consider two of them. The first is the method offered by Rudolph Glauber who wrote extensively upon alchemical matters. This was done by the use of his salt which is still referred to as Glauber's Salts, also known as Sal Mirabilis and acknowledged by modern medicine as a mild laxative; although Glauber makes it quite clear that this salt has great power to make accessible the healing power of the mineral kingdoms.

Firstly this salt must be prepared as it is a key to open the doors of the 'King's Palace.' If we gently drop small amounts of sulphuric acid onto sea salt, the reaction will create hydrogen chloride, also known as spirit of salt. This will manifest as a gas which will bubble over into the collection flask which should have distilled water in.

Collect this water as it has become hydrochloric acid and is highly corrosive. Be very careful that it does not come into contact with sensitive areas of the body: one must wear goggles and protective clothing, such as a mask, when handling acids and other unstable and dangerous substances. The salt in the flask is now collected from the flask and placed in a new flask to which distilled water is added and the salt then re-crystallized from the water. This must be done several times. The salt will now look like crushed ice and will melt at a low temperature. Dry the crystals gently and they will become pure white in colour and ready for use.

For this method the alchemist takes one part gold and nine parts of the salt. The salt is placed in a crucible and is heated to melting point to which the gold is then added as filings or gold leaf. Now the alchemist adds small pieces of charcoal that has been made from oak or, better still, vine prunings, as these two materials will have a high salt content which is ideal for our work. Continue with the heating of the material for twenty minutes and then pour out onto a hot metal dish. This, as Glauber says, is the 'Golden Carbuncle that shines in the night like a burning coal.' However you will notice that the mass has turned a deep red colour owing to the gold and all is now ground exceedingly fine. This is now placed in a flask and covered with strong mercury which has been circulated over its honey, and is then left to digest for a month somewhere warm; alternatively it can be circulated in the pelican too. The mercury becomes red in colour as it absorbs the properties of the gold, whilst the residue can be saved for further work. One drop of this tincture in wine or water daily will be a sufficient dosage to imbibe to release the potency thereof.

Mademoiselle Grimaldi's Aurum Potable

Writing in the 18th century the French alchemist and chemist, Nicolas Lemery gave the following formula for the creation of a Potable Gold which has been favoured by many alchemists ever since. Basically this is one of the more accessible formulae that exists and is not a difficult work to perform. However there is some danger in the sense that the alchemist is working with two extremely dangerous acids, hydrochloric and nitric acid both of which can cause serious injuries and must be treated with extreme care at all times to avoid mishap. Therefore the use of protective eyewear and gloves is essential, as are stout shoes. Owing to the nature of this working it is best done outside in a well-ventilated area because of the fumes and toxins that arise from the acids, which under no circumstances must you breathe them in, as the fumes will cause pulmonary damage and create breathing problems. On a practical note if the working is outside and there is a spillage of the acids then they are less likely to damage any fabrics and furniture.

Therefore, in the name of God, mix 45ml of hydrochloric acid with 15ml nitric acid; thus creating an aqua regia, 'The King's Water'. This will dissolve our gold which will allow us access to its power. In a separate flask place a gram of finely divided gold, the gold being as pure as you can get, and gently pour over the gold our aqua regia; this will fume a little so take care.

Note: Do not add gold to the aqua regia as it can burst into flames. Pour the acid carefully on to the gold.

The solution will turn a deep yellow colour as the sulphur of the gold is released. The alchemist now pours it into a separating funnel to which is then added 30ml of rosemary oil, which of course is a vegetable oil of the sun, and the mixture is left to stand.

The rosemary oil will now float over the aqua regia and the two will not mix as the oil will absorb the gold as the aqua regia will lose its colour and the rosemary oil becomes yellow. The two are now to be separated by the use of the separating funnel with the aqua regia flowing out and leaving the rosemary oil behind. The oil is now to be placed in a clean flask and covered with 150mls of our vegetable mercury which has been assiduously prepared as the arte demands.

Let this flask now stand somewhere warm and undisturbed for a month after which it can be decanted and stored in a dark bottle. It will have a purple colour and a pleasant taste; this is Mademoiselle Grimaldi's Aurum Potable. One drop in wine or water daily will grant access to the power of the healing power of Helios the sun, from whom all good things come.

CHAPTER FOURTEEN

Urania: Ingress into the Lapis Philosophorum

Urine is a powerful substance unappreciated and dismissed by all, except for the wise, who know something of its nature, and will think differently about it. Apart from its power to make plants grow luxuriantly, owing to its nitrate content (but it will also burn them too if highly concentrated), it can also heal and promote wellbeing. But more importantly, it is a route to the fabled Philosopher's Stone and the red and white powders of transmutation. This is acknowledged in some alchemical texts whereby it is said that the Stone can be created from 'Our First Matter' which is then described as something which we all know of but is thrown away without any further appreciation of its value and what it can do. Firstly I will consider healing menstrums created from one's urine and secondly a means of ingress into the realm of the Philosopher's Stone.

When working with urine there are two important points to take into consideration. Firstly the alchemist will need to have a low salt diet for a few days to lower the sodium levels in their urine, and secondly they will need to have drunk red wine the day previously as this will produce a urine which is suitable for the work. As urine has been through a live body it is deemed to be 'philosophical' that is, been touched by the life spirit and contains something thereof, thus making it suitable for our works. The average human will excrete about 1.5 litres of urine in a twenty-four hour period, which, if it is collected starting when one wakes up in the morning and then throughout the day, will give sufficient for our works. Urine is 95% water with 3% urea, the rest being made up of various waste products that the body cannot assimilate, but it does carry a large amount of life force, your life force, and it thus has a natural sympathy with you and your vibrations, and with this fact it becomes a useful ally in our works.

Figure 26: Urine distillation

Healing menstrums:

Whilst it is not uncommon within some schools of thought that the drinking of one's urine is good for health such activity within the western mindset is considered to be abhorrent. Yet in the alchemical world urine is seen as a menstrum that will cleanse the body of toxins and will also help to alleviate arthritis. It is also viewed as something which will generally promote one's health and wellbeing. As urine is sterile when it leaves the body, we need to break it down before we can work with it, and, remembering how alchemy claims that our work starts 'in darkness and in death', we leave it to ferment. This is the key which unlocks the doors to the alchemical kingdoms. Therefore we place our flask of urine somewhere dark and warm; it is then left there for forty days and nights. The urine is covered so that neither dust nor any dirt may enter therein and can pollute our 'Prima Materia.'

After this time it will have gone from being clear and clean-looking to a darkened smelly putrefying mess. This is our matter starting to break down and is a good sign that it is now ready for distillation. Pour the urine into a large flask and distil it at a low temperature similar to that needed for the distillation of the wine spirit, however be sure to save 200ml as we will need to imbibe our salts with this in due course. When we are distilling the urine we do not want the temperature too hot, no more than 100°c, as this will destroy the life force in the urine which we want. Collect the first third that distils over; this will be the most volatile part of the urine and is the mercury which contains the spirit. With the low temperature this may take a week to perform, so do not rush it. Any salts that volatilise and collect in the top of the flask need to be collected and kept, these are the volatile salts of the 16c alchemist Van Helmont who prized them for their great healing potentials. The volatised salts are our sulphur; collect the volatile salts and the mercury which distilled over and keep them separate. The remains are now poured into a large dish and evaporated to dryness; the distilled urine is then poured back over and redistilled off, this is done several times as it will enrich the mercury considerably. The remains are now collected from the dish and calcined to whiteness and the salt is leached out as our arte demands and whose modus we are now familiar with. These salts can also be left out at night, like the plant salts, prior to being used. When calcining the remains, do this outside and away from people as it stinks most foul and do not stand downwind from it either. When you have the whitened salts that you have extracted from the calcined remains, add more of the urine which we kept back, digest it for a day and a night and re-calcine. This is repeated again and we then collect our white salt. From the urine which we have distilled, this is our mercury; the volatile salts which collected in the helm, our sulphur, and the fixed white salts from the calcined remains of the urine, these are our three essentials.

Figure 27: Volatile salts of urine

Taking both our salts, the volatile and the fixed, we place them in a flask and pour over them our mercury and seal the flask which is then left to digest in the warm and dark. After forty days and nights, our philosophical month, we can distil off and bottle our healing nostrum; a few drops daily are considered to be a great aid to health and wellbeing.

Figure 28: The dry distillation of urine salts

Lapis Alba et Ruba

The arte allows for the confection of the red and white stones which will perform transmutations of a high order. We will now consider how traditional alchemical techniques have been used in the past to perform this work. As with the previous work we collect our urine over a twenty-four hour period and follow the same protocols of diet that were demanded for the work. Again it is left to ferment, however as this working is of a higher nature, prayers for the success thereof must proceed first. It will also be conducive to success if you also wait until the moon favours the sun with a trine and the moon is waxing too. On the day when the degree on the ascendant is the same as the day that you were born, we can proceed with the distillations. As the zodiac turns through all twelve signs during a twenty-four hour period the degree on the ascendant changes every four minutes, therefore at some point in the day the degree on the ascendant will be the same as when you were born. Therefore, as this is a personal work with one's own urine for a high goal, it seems quite obvious that this is the most optimum time for you to work, even invocations of the angel who governs this degree in your natal chart would not go amiss. If you do not know your birth chart then this will not be applicable to you however you can still work with the moon/sun trine and a general invocation to Hermes for assistance and blessing upon your workings.

Figure 29: Fixed salt of urine

Distil slowly, no more than 80°c, and let the most volatile part of the urine sweat over gently; for this operation use a retort and be mindful that it may take a week, or even ten days or so. Collect the first 250mls that distils over, this is the most volatile part and is our mercury. As before collect any volatile salts that come over in the beak of the retort. The remains are gently evaporated until they become a stinking black tar, and the distillate that we kept is to be poured back over this and gently allowed to circulate, therefore you will need an aludel attached to the flask. Let this mercury circulate for fourteen days and nights, ideally from the new until the full moon; this will allow our mercury to be enriched. After this the remains are dried off and calcined, to these ashes we add another 500ml of fermented urine which we have saved and did not distil. Again we distil this off and need not keep, the remains again are calcined and the white salts extracted according to arte. We now have our distilled volatile urine, the volatile white salt and the fixed salts from the calcinations.

Figure 30: Calcination of salts on an open fire

Combine both salts and to these add the 250ml of the volatile part of the urine which we distilled off earlier. Then we need to re-distil this off the salts, very gently as we did before; however do not distil to dryness but leave sufficient urine to keep the salts just moist. Gather the salts and re-calcine them again, then add the distilled urine to the salts as previously. Distil off the urine as before and re-calcine the salts again; this operation needs to be done three times until crystals appear; these crystals are to be collected as they are our purified sulphur. The urine is distilled three times, each time leaving the last tenth behind, thus only collecting the most volatile parts, this is our mercury. We now have our mercury, sulphur and salt, the salt and sulphur are added together and crushed very fine, they are now placed in a flask and a little of the mercury is added, only a little as it does not want to be drowned. Seal the flask and digest it at 40°c for a philosophical month then add a little more of the mercury and again digest for a further month as previously.

This feeding with mercury and digestion can go on for a year as the salts will eventually turn into a waxy solid. The waxy solid will turn black, which is the nigredo stage of the work. When this happens the heat is slightly raised and the digestion continues. Leave it quietly to mature as the colours now change; the peacock's tail becomes visible as the salts turn a bluish colour before turning white. When the salts are white they are considered toxic and need to be seeded with either gold or silver depending whether you are creating a red or white stone.

The white salts are now our unfermented white stone which will need to be divided into three parts, the first third is used for multiplication and this is done by grinding it fine and adding fresh urine and leaving it to digest. It will turn black then white as this operation can take three months to perform.

Our second third will create the white stone and will need to be fermented with silver. To do this take very fine silver and grind it with the white stone so both are as fine as you can produce them. They are then placed into a flask and imbibed with a small amount of our mercury as previously performed. Then they are left to digest as before and they eventually will turn black and then white. This white stage indicates the completion of the work.

With the last third we will create the red stone; this can be achieved by taking the stone and sealing it in a flask. The flask must be kept hot enough so that the stone will stay molten for a month. At this point the stone will turn orange and when it does is to be cooled off slowly. When it is cooled we then reheat and bring the temperature up to 250°c at which point the stone will turn to red powder. It is now ready to be fermented with gold. The gold must be pure 24k and must be reduced to very fine particles. The stone is now added to the fine gold and both ground together. Place them in a flask, and as previously performed, add a little of the mercury to the stone and digest in a gentle heat. This will cause the stone to turn black and then white and eventually red, thus the stone is complete. Whilst a few grains can be taken internally and used as a medicine for rejuvenation it is also considered to have the power to transmute base metal into gold.

Traditionally if a little of the white stone is wrapped in beeswax and dropped into either molten lead or tin will transmute the metal into silver; whilst a few grains of the red stone, projected as previously done into either molten lead or mercury, would cause the metal to transmute into gold. Thus the work is complete, however if everyone can make gold *'who will bake the bread'?*

ORA ET LABORA

Figure 31: The Crowning of the Work

Essential Reading

Kirchwegar, Dr. Anton J. The Golden Chain of Homer

Laport, J. Erik & Gabrielsson, Dr. Roger Cracking the Philosopher's Stone

Hollandus, Johann Urania

        Opera Vegetablis

        The Work on Wine

Glauber, Rudolph Secret Fire of the Philosophers

Plimer, Robert Anderson Decoding Alchemy

Heliophilus Alchemy Rising: The Green Book

Rubaphilos, Salfluere The Hermes Paradigm

Waite, A.E. Hermetic & Alchemical Writings of Paracelsus the Great

Bartlett, Robert Allen Real Alchemy: The Way of the Crucible

Frater Albertus The Alchemist's Handbook

Junius, Manfred The Practical Handbook of Plant Alchemy

Barbault, Armand Gold of a Thousand Mornings

See also the following French alchemical film with subtitles whereby an actual transmutation takes place: vimeo.com/16322285

Index

A
Aqua Angelus 31, 59, 62
Aquarius 68, 69
Aries 30, 66, 68, 69

B
Bhasma 108, 109

C
Cancer 68, 69
Capricorn 68, 69
Chymical Wedding. 19, 20, 31, 81
Circulatum Minor 100, 101, 105, 107
Culpeper 37, 72

D
dew 30, 49, 50, 66

E
elemental Archeus 70
Emerald Tablet 31

F
fennel 29, 84, 101
Fixed Mercury 59
Franz Bardon 70

G
Fulcanelli 10

G
Gemini 66, 68, 69
George Starkey . 59, 60, 61
Gold 50, 114, 116, 128

H
Hollandus 7, 52, 78, 79, 128

I
Israel Regardie 7, 13

J
Jung 17
Junius 7, 13, 105, 128
Jupiter 71, 72, 97, 99

K
Kabbalah 7, 18, 24

L
lavender 29, 99
Leo 68, 69
Liber Mutus 30, 66
Libra 68, 69
Luna 71, 72, 98, 103

M

Mars 71, 72, 98
Mercury 20, 54
mugwort......84, 86, 87, 98

O

Oleum Tartari....50, 96, 97
Ouroboros..................... 83

P

Paracelsus....7, 18, 19, 20, 22, 95, 128
Philalethes 59
Philosopher's Stone 13, 100, 118, 128
Pisces..................... 68, 69
planetary ens 95, 98
planetary hour 72, 75, 77, 101, 104
planetary tinctures. 71, 77
Plant stones 34, 78, 79, 100
Primum Ens........... 50, 95

R

Red King 89, 114
rosemary....29, 81, 84, 98, 101, 104, 117
Rudolph Glauber 114, 115, 128

S

Sagittarius 68, 69
Salt 21, 58
Saturn.............. 71, 72, 99
Scorpio................... 68, 69
Star of Basil 91, 94
Sulphur.................. 21, 56
Sun 28, 71, 72, 98, 114

T

Taurus 30, 66, 69
Terra Damnata....... 20, 58
thyme..................... 29, 84

U

Urine.................. 118, 119

V

Valentinus..................... 22
Van Helmont... 59, 60, 61, 62, 81, 90, 93, 120
Venus................ 71, 72, 99
Virgo 69

W

White Queen 26, 89
Wine stone 90, 91, 94
Wine tartar................... 90

www.ingramcontent.com/pod-product-compliance
Lightning Source LLC
Chambersburg PA
CBHW030235170426
43201CB00006B/225